THE NON-ELECTRIC LIGHTING SERIES

BOOK 6: Kerosene Pressure Lanterns

Ron Brown

Newark Valley, New York

Notice: This manual is designed to provide information on kerosene-burning lamps and lanterns that employ a mantle.

It is not the purpose of this guide to reprint all the information that is otherwise available, but to complement, amplify, and supplement other texts and resources. You are urged to read all the available material and learn as much as you can about kerosene mantle lamps and lanterns and to tailor the information to your specific circumstances.

Every effort has been made to make this guide as complete and accurate as possible. However, there may be mistakes, both typographical and in content. Therefore this text should be used only as a general guide and not as the ultimate source of pressure lantern information. Furthermore, this guide contains information that is current only up to the printing date.

The purpose of this manual is to educate and entertain. The views, opinions, positions, and strategies expressed by the author are his alone. The author makes no representations as to the accuracy, completeness, correctness, suitability, or validity of any information in this book and will not be liable for any errors, omissions, or delays in this information or any losses, injuries, or damages arising from its use.

ISBN 978-0-9905564-8-0

Published by
R&C Publishing
15 Dr. Knapp Road South
Newark Valley, NY 13811

Printed in the United States of America

THE NON-ELECTRIC LIGHTING SERIES
BOOK 6: Kerosene Pressure Lanterns
Table of Contents

FOREWORD

When Ron first approached me about writing this foreword, I had to admit that my own knowledge was less than perfect when it came to pressure lanterns. Sure, I knew that Coleman made lanterns and that there are hundreds of used ones on eBay as well as newer models in sporting goods stores. I also knew that Coleman has been making lanterns for years and that parts are still available for most if not all models.

That being said, this book helped educate me about *kerosene* lanterns. In *Kerosene Pressure Lanterns*, Ron teaches us about the specific Coleman models that burn kerosene (there are only a few). He also explains how to convert some specific Coleman gas-fueled models to kerosene. This is good stuff.

But there is a world out there beyond Coleman. Did you know that outside the U.S., Coleman lanterns are actually outnumbered by Petromax, a pressure lantern of German design? It, too, is a *kerosene* pressure lantern. As a matter of fact, the Petromax heyday was before World War II but Petromax brand lanterns are still being made along with a multitude of off-brand clones.

In this book, Ron discusses Petromax design issues along with myths and advertising hype. This is good to know because both Coleman and Petromax lanterns generate light on par with a 100 or 200 or 300-watt light bulb depending on the model.

I must also confess that before reading this book, I also knew very little, if anything about Aladdin table lamps. I knew what they looked like but not much more. Now I know that Aladdins are mantle lamps that burn kerosene. They are not pressurized so they don't hiss or flicker. They produce up to 60 watts-worth of smooth white light and they have been on the market over a hundred years, since 1909 to be exact.

Aladdins have a cult following and there is even a worldwide collectors club, The Aladdin Knights of the Mystic Light. And, as with many of the Colemans, you can buy them brand new as well as used. I am surprised that in spite of my many years of prepping I somehow never heard much about them.

Kerosene Pressure Lanterns is not a book you are likely to sit down and read cover-to-cover in one sitting. Because it covers a lot of ground, you will want to digest it, page by page, chapter by chapter. My guess is that you will read, browse, and turn to it later for reference purposes. Just do not be surprised if, after reading it, you start searching out a kerosene lamp of your own and quite possibly an Aladdin. That is what I am doing.

One more thing. It has it dawned on me that what Ron Brown is doing throughout his entire Non-Electric Lighting Series is documenting knowledge from yesteryear that might otherwise be forgotten. To take things one step further, this is knowledge that may be needed down the road if our reliance on electricity becomes compromised. It could happen, you know.

For that reason, I think it would be wise to have this set of books tucked away in your reference library. One thing for certain is that they are priced right – even downright cheap. As I like to say, knowledge is power and the information in this book, as well as the others in the series, is powerful stuff.

Gaye Levy
September 2015

"Let there be light." – Genesis 1:3

INTRODUCTION

This book covers pressure lanterns that burn kerosene.

Judging by eBay listings, some people think that Coleman lanterns (*all* Coleman lanterns) burn kerosene. They do not. The vast majority burn white gas (also known as Coleman fuel), NOT kerosene.

Just to keep things interesting, however, a few Coleman models exist that DO burn kerosene.

So let's start again. This book covers pressure lanterns that burn kerosene. In the USA, that translates into a few Coleman models in addition to lanterns of the (German) Petromax design.

In the USA, Coleman is top dog. Worldwide, however, more Petromax lanterns exist than do Coleman. Dozens of Petromax lanterns (and Petromax clones bearing different brand names) are available on eBay at any given time.

This book is aimed at USA-preppers and USA-survivalists. Hence, NOT covered in this book are lanterns that are NOT of the Coleman or Petromax design, that are NOT sold in the USA, or for which spare parts are NOT available. (How's that for a quadruple negative?) Point is, Tilley (English), Vapalux (formerly English but now Korean), Optimus (Swedish), and Austramax (Australian) do not appear in this book.

NOTE: As we speak, just as this book is going to press, Lehman's has begun carrying the Austramax (www.lehmans.com).

But even without Tilley and Vapalux and Optimus and Austramax there's a lot of ground to cover:

- **Theory.** A bit of pressure lantern theory will be discussed – mantles, fuels, generators, etc.

- **Coleman Kerosene.** And we'll identify various Coleman models that ARE designed for kerosene. We'll ignore collectibles (expensive) and orphans (no spare parts).

- **Conversions.** We'll also learn how to convert several Coleman gas models to kerosene (what generator to use and so on).

- **Petromax.** Another section deals with Petromax. Petromax is both a design and a brand. It's a confusing topic and the marketplace is bristling with hustlers.

- **Safety.** BriteLyt (a USA-branded Petromax clone) advertises that its lanterns are safe using gasoline as well as kerosene. If so, BriteLytes would be unique in human history. We'll discuss.

- **Diesel.** Petromax lanterns will burn diesel fuel. Plus we'll identify some Coleman models that can burn diesel.

- **Aladdin.** And we'll cover Aladdin lamps. They are mantle lamps. And they burn kerosene. But they are not pressure lamps. Just gotta sneak 'em in here somewhere.

Interesting tidbits are sprinkled throughout. How to improvised a preheat cup. Substituting a wire mesh globe for glass. If you come across an old lantern, how do you know if kerosene is the intended fuel? Stuff like that.

THEORY

Generators

In the context of pressure lanterns, the term 'generator' confuses people. Having been raised in the age of electricity, when someone says 'generator,' what jumps to mind is a complex mass of windings, brushes, and capacitors.

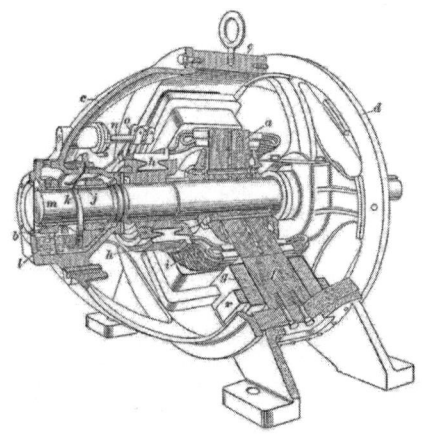

■ **ABOVE:** *An electrical generator, cutaway view. "D.-C. Motors and Generators" by Scott Hancock, 1941, page 36* ■

So let's demystify. To do so, we must return to Eighth Grade science. If you remember, we need three things for a fire: (1) fuel, (2) oxygen, and (3) kindling temperature.

But before fuel will combine with oxygen and ignite, it must be in a gaseous state. Liquid fuel must be converted to a gas so that it can mix with gaseous oxygen. In the lantern world, that's the purpose of the generator. To take liquid fuel and convert it to gaseous fuel. To 'generate' a gas from a liquid.

A steam jenny (in the steam-engine world) performs a similar function. 'Jenny' is slang for generator. A steam generator 'generates' gaseous steam from liquid water. A simple teakettle is a steam jenny.

And the generator for a Coleman lantern is little more than a length of brass tubing. Liquid fuel enters one end of the tube (under pressure that we pumped into the fuel tank). Heat is applied to the outside of the tube. The liquid inside the tube boils and turns to a gas. Gaseous fumes exit the other end of the tube. Gas (in the 'solid-liquid-gas' sense of things) has been generated from a liquid.

■ **ABOVE:** *The Q77, an early generator circa World War I. If the tip plugged, the lantern had to be shut down, allowed to cool, and the generator removed for cleaning.* ■

■ **ABOVE:** *A generator for today's Coleman 639C kerosene lantern. The hook on the West end attaches to an eccentric block inside the lantern. Turning a 'cleaning lever' on the lantern causes the rod to travel back and forth inside the generator. The East end of the rod has a needle or 'pricker' that cleans out the tip. The pricker can be activated while the lantern is running.* ■

A generator with a filter (which is what gas lanterns have) will, on kerosene, gradually plug. Could you use it a few evenings to get through a blackout? Sure (assuming you have the right tip size and so forth). But sooner or later a lantern with a filter in its generator will, on kerosene, refuse to run.

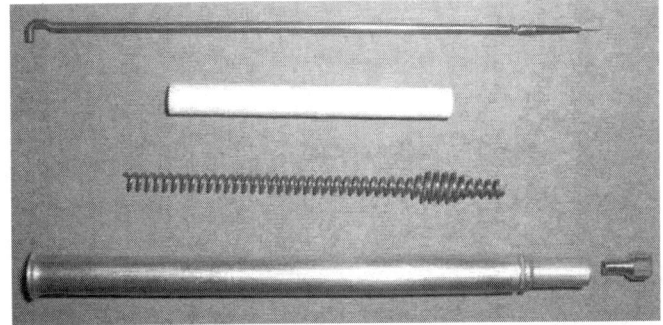

■ **ABOVE:** *This is a 200A (gas) generator. At the bottom is the outer barrel and tip. At the top is the cleaning rod/pricker. Below the pricker is an asbestos cylinder (filter). Below the filter is a "spring." Sizes and shapes may vary, but all Coleman Instant-Lite gas lanterns have these five components.* ■

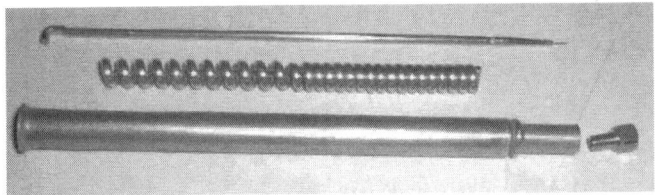

■ **ABOVE:** *This is a 201 (kerosene) generator. A spring (only) replaces the spring-plus-filter found in gas lanterns.* ■

Mantles

With candles, olive oil lamps, and kerosene wick-type lamps, the light by which we see is produced by a flame. Mantle lamps are different.

Just as a tungsten filament in an electric bulb 'incandesces' or glows from the heat of the electric current passing through the wire, so a mantle in a non-electric lamp incandesces from a flame's heat. The light produced by the mantle is many times brighter than the light from the flame itself.

A 1922 Coleman ad said their mantles were made from "long-fibre Egyptian cotton" although cotton has been superseded by rayon.

The woven cloth mantle is soaked in a rare-earth solution, then coated with lacquer. It's the rare earth that glows and produces light. The cloth is only a carrier. Before using the mantle the first time, we burn away the lacquer and cloth. The ash skeleton left behind is what incandesces and generates light.

Throughout most of the 1900's, thorium was the rare earth used in mantles. Thorium, however, is faintly radioactive (making it a hot-button issue). In the politically-correct 1980's, thorium mantles were largely (not totally) replaced with yttrium, a rare earth that is not radioactive.

Please know that old-time thorium mantles do burn brighter and hotter than the newer yttrium mantles. And old-time Coleman-brand thorium mantles are still available on eBay. Thorium mantles are not illegal to buy, sell, own, make, or use.

Kerosene requires more heat (hotter mantles) than does Coleman fuel. Many lantern conversions (where we run kerosene in a Coleman lantern designed for gas) require the hotter-burning thorium mantles; the newer yttrium mantles aren't quite up to the task.

You do need to use some common sense with thorium mantles. You should not eat them. In fact, you may want to wash your hands after installing them rather than licking your fingers.

■ **ABOVE:** *All Coleman mantles branded 'Silk-Lite' are of the old thorium type and are no longer made. Pictured here is a Silk-Lite No. 21A that would have been used before 1980. Today, thorium Silk-Lites are available on eBay.* ■

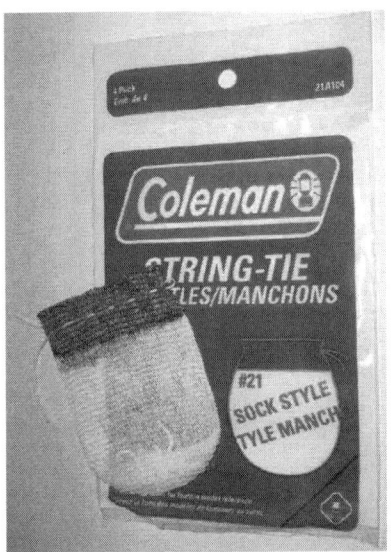

■ **ABOVE:** *The yttrium #21 (what Walmart sells today) replaced the thorium Silk-Lite No. 21A.* ■

Next, how about Petromax mantles?

Personally, I don't like them. Petromax mantles are round, rather than egg-shaped like Coleman. But regardless of what shape they have or what brand name they carry (BriteLyt, Butterfly, Primus, etc.) they are too delicate, too fragile for my taste. So I'm giving them short shrift, sorry. I'll let someone else carry that banner and argue the intricacies thereof.

I can give Petromax mantles that kind of curt brushoff (fortunately) because Coleman mantles work just fine on Petromax lanterns. Coleman #11 mantles work well on a big 500CP Petromax. Coleman #21 mantles work well on a 150CP Petromax.

Next up, Lancaster and Peerless mantles, a case study in their own right. First, however, we need to understand sizes.

In the thorium world of yesteryear, Coleman sizes (small to large) were Silk-Lite No. 20, Silk-Lite No. 21A, Silk-Lite No. 999, and Silk-Lite No. 1111.

In today's yttrium world, the corresponding Coleman sizes (small to large) are #20, #21, #99, and #11.

In 2007, a Philippine company called the Coleman Mantle Mfg. Corp. (that had worked with Coleman under various licensing agreements since World War II) changed hands and became the Gasman Mantle Mfg. Corp.

Both Gasman and its predecessor produced Peerless (brand) and Lancaster (brand) mantles. On-line browsing reveals users to be quite enthusiastic about Peerless mantles; most people consider them superior to Coleman. The Peerless size equivalent to a Coleman #21 is the '2C-HG.' The Peerless size equivalent to a Coleman #99 is a

'24-A.' The Peerless size equivalent to a Coleman #11 is a 'Type 111.'

Printed on the pre-Gasman **Peerless** packets was the message "*Made for European and American Markets.*" That, I believe, was a roundabout way of announcing Peerless mantles were yttrium. To my knowledge, thorium mantles were not allowed for sale in Europe. Today, the 'European' phrase has disappeared.

Printed on the pre-Gasman **Lancaster** packets was the message, "They emit a very small amount of radioactivity whether lit or unlit." Today, under Gasman, that phrase, too, has disappeared.

WARN *j*

These mantles are perfectly safe and satisfactory when used as intended and according to lantern instructions. However, they emit a very small amount of radioactivity whether lit or unlit. Therefore:

* *Do not inhale the mantle smoke or ingest mantle ash.*
* *Dispose of ash in trash. Do not handle mantles for...*

So, today, we have (1) new Gasman Peerless mantles, (2) old pre-Gasman Peerless mantles, (3) new Gasman Lancaster mantles, and (4) old pre-Gasman Lancaster mantles.

Which ones are thorium?

Legitimate question. Thorium mantles do burn hotter than yttrium and are necessary, in many cases, to properly vaporize kerosene. And kerosene is the subject of this book.

I emailed Sam Blank, the owner of Gasman. He was gracious enough to respond but, unfortunately, after a few emails I found myself still puzzled on the thorium issue.

It finally dawned on me that, for me at least, performance (getting kerosene to vaporize properly) is my primary concern. I'm not overly concerned about thorium or yttrium or radioactivity. (See the next section entitled *Mantle Radioactivity*.) If anything in Gasman's Peerless-Lancaster lineup is hot-burning thorium, it is likely Lancaster. And the only *size* that Lancaster sells (at least that I'm aware of) is the 24-A.

So here's how it checked out:

- A big Coleman Model 237 kerosene lantern will run kerosene on a #11 mantle (yttrium) but requires a Silk-Lite No. 1111 (thorium) to run diesel. *But it will also run diesel on a Gasman Lancaster 24-A.* [It flares up if you attempt to run diesel on a Gasman *Peerless* 24-A.]

- When we get to 'conversions' (i.e. converting gas lanterns to run on kero), we find the Coleman Model 335 (given a 339 generator) will run kerosene on a #21 mantle (yttrium) but requires a Silk-Lite No. 21A mantle (thorium) to run diesel. *But it will also run diesel on a Gasman Lancaster 24-A.* [It carbons up after half an hour if you attempt to run diesel on a Gasman *Peerless* 24-A.]

In short, the Lancaster 24-A can be substituted for either a Silk-Lite No. 1111 (thorium) on the big side or a Silk-Lite No. 21A (thorium) on the small side. By design or coincidence, the Lancaster 24-A is a midsize compromise.

And is the Gasman Lancaster 24-A itself thorium? To me, that becomes a moot point, a 'who cares?' *Performance* is what we seek and the Lancaster 24-A delivers.

The 24-A is, physically, quite large (see image below). You may need to tie it onto the burner tube, above the grooved burner screen where it ordinarily fastens. If it touches the preheater cup during its initial firing it can glue itself to the metal, producing a hole and destroying itself.

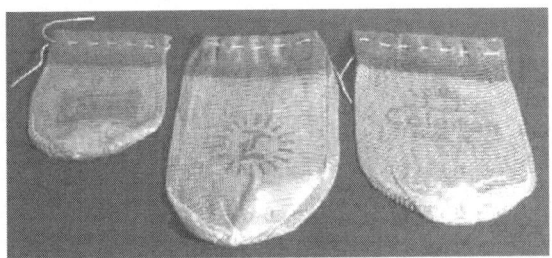

■ **ABOVE (Left to Right):** *Coleman Silk-Lite No. 21A; Lancaster 24-A; Coleman Silk-Lite No. 1111.* ■

Please understand that what Gasman (or anybody else) makes today is not necessarily what they'll be making next year. Formulas and government rules and management philosophy are all subject to change.

If you want to stock up on mantles ahead of coming hard times, I suggest you buy a few and do your own hands-on testing. Make sure they do what you need for them to do. Then buy more from the same seller. Don't sink your money in a hoard of mantles based on what somebody else says, be it on-line or in a book (even this book). Check 'em out yourself, up close and personal. You'll sleep better.

FYI. After a few rewrites I asked Sam Blank to review what I had composed (above) on the topic of Peerless, Lancaster, thorium, etc. He responded with this: "The article in my opinion is as good as it can get, you have my approval on it."

Mantle Radioactivity

In emphasizing performance I don't want to come across as flippant about the dangers of radioactivity in regard to mantles. But exactly how 'radioactive' is *radioactive*? It needs to be put in context.

A 'Roentgen Equivalent in Man' (abbreviated rem) is a measure of radiation. A millirem (abbreviated mrem) = $^{1}/_{1000}$ rem.

Ramsar, Iran has the world's highest background radiation with some houses receiving 36 mrem per day. That's the *daily* mrem equivalent of the *annual* 132 mSv (milliSieverts) cited on-line. http://ecolo.org/documents/documents_in_english/ramsar-natural-radioactivity/ramsar.html.

For most of us, located at a distance from Ramsar, background radiation is around one mrem per day, not 36.

A dental X-ray is equivalent to 0.5 mrem. A mammogram is equivalent to 300 mrem.

The Nuclear Regulatory Commission publication *Systematic Radiological Assessment of Exemptions for Source and Byproduct Materials (NUREG-1717)* estimates that 'avid campers' (making 26 two-day camping trips per year, loading the car, riding in the car, changing mantles, etc., and using Coleman-type lanterns **with thorium mantles**) receive 0.05 to 6 mrem per year. http://www.nrc.gov/reading-rm/doc-collections/nuregs/staff/sr1717/nureg-1717.pdf

Let's sidestep all the tongue-twisters and express this in more familiar units: dollars.

Background radiation is $1 per day.

Eating a banana is 10¢ additional. A dental X-ray is 50¢. A flight from New York to Los Angeles is $4. A mammogram is $300.

An 'avid camper' would receive $365 per year in background radiation plus somewhere between 5¢ and $6 per year from thorium mantles. Unless the camper in question lived in Ramsar, Iran, in which case background radiation alone would be $13,000 per year.

Hopefully this helps quantify the risk posed by thorium mantles. There is a risk but, in my opinion, the operative word is *small*.

Firing

■ **ABOVE:** *New mantles are flexible. Pictured here are 'sock style' mantles, resembling miniature drawstring bags. There is only one opening. It's at the top; it fits over the end of the burner tube. The mantles are hand-tied in place. Sometimes the factory-installed drawstring breaks. In that case, you can replace the drawstring with a piece of fine wire. Once fired, the mantle is rigid and pretty well stays in position all by itself.* ■

New mantles must be 'fired' before they will produce light. The factory-applied lacquer must be burned off. All that remains after firing is the ash of the cloth carrier and the rare earth. As you can imagine, mantles are rather delicate creatures.

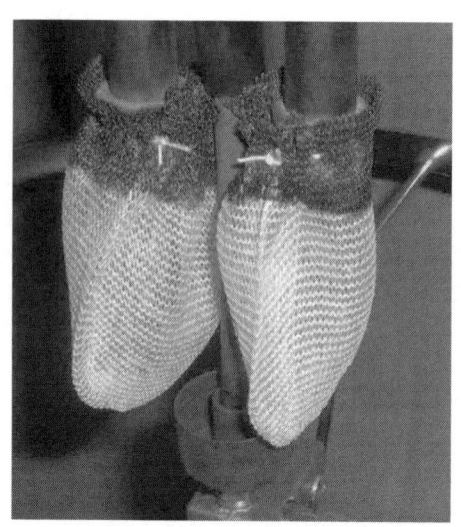

■ **ABOVE:** *New mantles mounted on a lantern, ready to be fired. They've been turned so that, after firing, they won't touch the generator.* ■

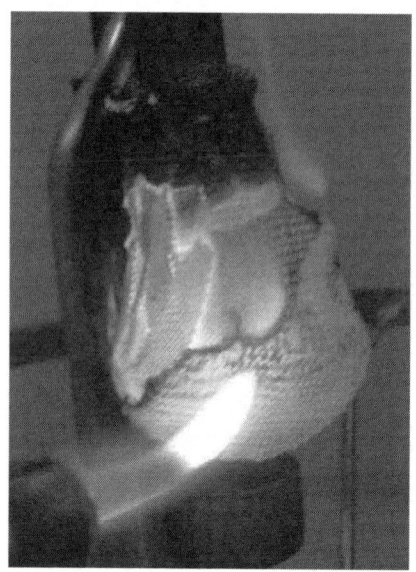

■ **ABOVE:** *A mantle being fired. You can see the flame from my torch.* ■

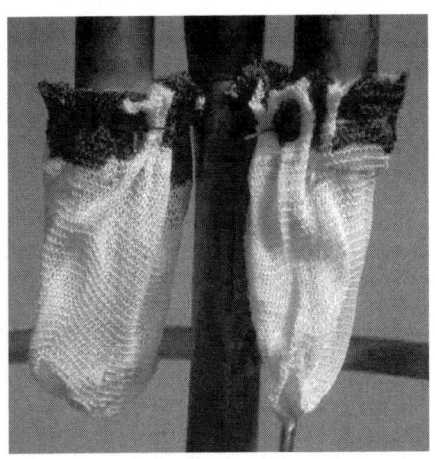

■ **ABOVE:** *Newly fired mantles are flaccid and limpy. It is recommended by one and all that firing be done outdoors so as to avoid inhaling the smoke (particularly with the older radioactive mantles). What nobody tells you, however, is that a mild breeze will break your newly fired mantles. It happens quickly, without warning. So 'outdoors' really means 'outdoors but sheltered from the wind.'* ■

■ **ABOVE:** *When you first turn on the pressurized fuel and light the newly-burned-off mantle, it puffs up like a tiny egg-shaped balloon and becomes rigid, holding its shape thereafter.* ■

Fuel

The lantern 'system' that produces light doesn't stop with the mechanical lantern itself. The system as a whole must include the fuel. No fuel = an incomplete system = no light.

In a kerosene pressure lantern, the fuel (as you might expect) is kerosene. In a gas pressure lantern, the fuel is white gas (Coleman fuel) or, in some instances, automobile gas.

The difference between 'gas' and 'kerosene' is that kerosene is *combustible* whereas gas is *flammable*.

'Flash point' is the lowest temperature at which a fuel will ignite in air. OSHA defines a *combustible* liquid as "any liquid having a flash point at or above 100° F." A *flammable* liquid has a flash point below 100° F.

A flammable liquid (gas) thus takes fire more easily than a combustible liquid (kero). Spill some kerosene and you make a mess; spill some gas and you burn down the house.

There is a hierarchy of petroleum fuels based on flammability. In refining, the five major 'fractions' of petroleum are [1] refinery gases (methane, ethane, propane, and butane), [2] gasoline, [3] kerosene, [4] diesel oil, and [5] residues.

The refinery gases (propane, etc.) are not part of this discussion on liquid-fuel lanterns.

The gasoline-kerosene-diesel list goes from thinnest and most volatile to thickest and hardest to ignite.

Mineral spirits is near the boundary of gasoline and kerosene; actually it's on the kerosene side of the street.

'Residues' includes solid paraffin wax and the like. So the five major fractions span gases, liquids, and solids. (Note that gasoline is not a gas in the solid-liquid-gas sense of things. 'Gas' is a liquid. Tricky stuff, language.) Mineral spirits is worth a special note. As lantern fuel, mineral spirits can be substituted for kerosene. This may contradict information you find on-line but, in fact, it is so.

Depending on grade, the flash point of kerosene ranges from 100° F to 150° F (per the Phillips 66 MSDS #682950 that you can view on-line: http://www.coastoil.com/MSDS/Phillips%2066%20(Conoc o)/Kerosene.pdf).

The MSDS sheets for seven different brands of mineral spirits – Sunnyside, RustOleum, Klean-Strip, Parks, Sherwin Williams, Kerr, and Ace (Barr) – show flash points ranging from 102° F to 109° F. The lowest is Sunnyside; the highest, Kerr.

The MSDS sheets for five different brands of **odorless** mineral spirits – Sunnyside, RustOleum, Klean-Strip, Parks, and ConocoPhillips – show flash points from 105° F to 127° F. The lowest is RustOleum; the highest, ConocoPhillips.

Based on flash point, mineral spirits is 'combustible.' Based on flash point, mineral spirits qualifies as kerosene. Based on flash point, mineral spirits can be substituted for kerosene in a lamp or lantern.

I would like to shut down any potential brouhaha on this topic before it begins. The Non-Electric Lighting Series (of which this book is part) contains a volume entitled *Book 3: Lamp Fuels*. The above discussion (on mineral spirits and flash point) is drawn from that book. The Foreword to *Lamp Fuels* says this:

> "An early draft of this book [*Lamp Fuels*], as the author notes, was reviewed by two petrochemical engineers, a college physics professor, and a chemical engineer. As it so happens, I am the physics professor in question. But that was my past career. Today I work in the oil and gas industry and have been in the industry for almost 20 years.
>
> "I want to assure the reader that the information presented in this book [*Lamp Fuels*] is accurate. The topics, written from a lamp-fuel and lantern-fuel point of view, have been simplified but with full confidence I can state that what is presented is correct."

So, to avoid any ambiguity, The Non-Electric Lighting Series was written by me, Ron Brown. The series includes *Book 3: Lamp Fuels* as well as the volume at hand, *Book 6: Kerosene Pressure Lanterns*. What I presented in *Book 3: Lamp Fuels* was correct. What I've just presented here is the same material which is equally correct.

Preheating

Let's say you spot an old lantern at a flea market but it's not a model you're familiar with. How can you tell if *gas* or *kerosene* is the intended fuel?

First answer. If it's an Instant-Lite, it is NOT a kerosene lantern. That covers 95% of all the Coleman's out there. And how do you know if it's Instant-Lite?

Answer. It will have a shutoff valve similar to the one pictured above. The Instant-Lite feature was what made Coleman famous. Instant-Lite spanned zillions of model numbers, sizes, shapes, and colors of lanterns. And ALL Instant-Lites are gas. NO Instant-Lites are kerosene.

Second answer. If it has a preheater cup, it's a kerosene lantern.

Gasoline vaporizes so readily that a preheater cup is not necessary. The Coleman Quick-Lite lamps of the 1920's didn't need a preheater cup. They required just two wooden matches. But that's not enough heat for kerosene.

Quick-Lites were followed by Instant-Lites. And Instant-Lites don't need a preheater cup. They use a special fuel-air tube at startup. But the Instant-Lite feature doesn't provide enough heat for kerosene.

So to get the heat they need for initial vaporization of the fuel, kerosene lanterns have preheater cups. The cup is

19

filled with alcohol and set alight. It takes about four minutes for the alcohol to burn down and vaporize the fuel inside the generator and get the lantern started but the cup itself becomes a distinctive telltale feature. No preheat cup means it's not a kerosene lantern.

■ **ABOVE:** *The preheater cup wraps around the generator.* ■

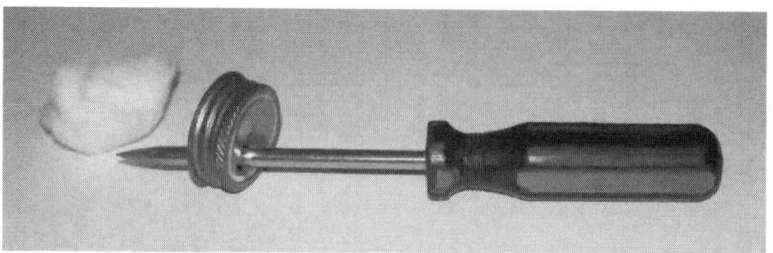

■ **ABOVE:** *Here's an improvised preheat cup. Punch a hole in a metal bottle cap. Mount the cap on the lantern's generator. If, at this point, you pour in alcohol, it will leak out. So stuff the bottle cap with a cotton puff. The cotton holds the alcohol; the cup holds the cotton. And use cotton, please. Synthetics melt. You'll have to clean out the charred cotton every few burns but it actually performs quite nicely.* ■

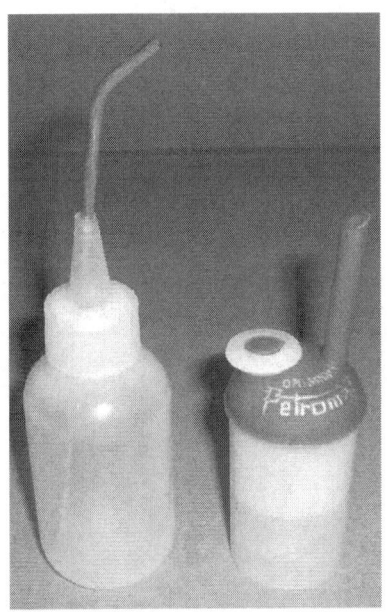

■ **ABOVE:** *Small plastic flasks are supplied by lantern manufacturers to squirt alcohol into the preheater cups. On the left is Coleman; on the right is Petromax. In all honesty, they don't work very well.* ■

■ **ABOVE:** *A million years ago, give or take, Coleman supplied metal alcohol or spirit bottles like this with their kerosene lanterns.* ■

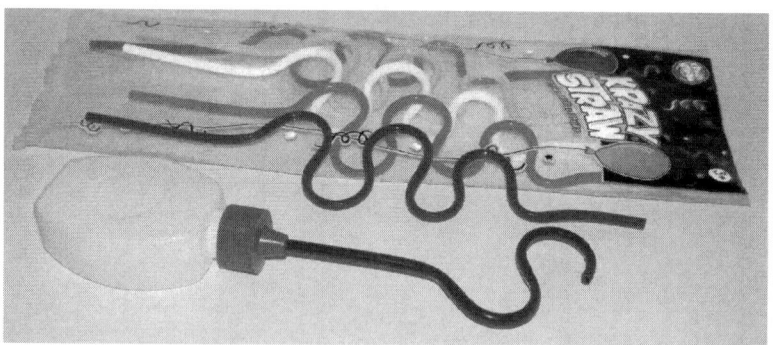

■ **ABOVE:** *You can fashion something similar out of Krazy Straws from the Dollar Store and a modern-day plastic squeeze bottle. Given a drill bit to enlarge a hole plus some gasket material or glue to stop a leak and you can fashion an alcohol bottle that works quite well.* ■

■ **ABOVE:** *This is what the bends and curly-Q's are all about.* ■

■ **ABOVE:** *This Coleman 214 has the globe and ventilator removed so you can see the preheater cup in action. After the alcohol has burned down (but before it goes out entirely), the fuel valve can be turned on. The lantern has been 'preheated.' That means the kerosene inside the generator is boiling and is in a gaseous state.* ■

■ **ABOVE:** *And this, Johnny, is why you should never light a liquid-fueled pressure lantern indoors. It's called a 'flare-up.'* **It's caused by insufficient preheating.** *Unfortunately, just about every YouTube video demonstrating 'how to light a lantern' shows the procedure taking place at the kitchen sink or on a cluttered workbench out in the shop. Now riddle me this. How will setting the kitchen curtains on fire in the middle of a blackout make life easier?* ■

No liquid-fuel pressure lantern is immune from flare-ups. Flare-ups are less frequent with gas-fueled lanterns (compared to kerosene lanterns) because gas is more volatile and vaporizes inside the generator more readily than kerosene. But flare-ups do happen with gas lanterns. Trust me.

Given a traditional Coleman design, should a flare-up occur, just turn off the fuel shutoff valve and be patient. The excess fuel will burn itself out and the flames will dwindle away. In fact, the flare-up might do your desired preheating; at the end of the flare-up, the lantern might actually settle down and operate properly. If so, turn the fuel back on and go about your business. (But really and truly, it's not the recommended way.)

With the Petromax design, flare-ups are more treacherous because there is no separate fuel shutoff valve. The Petromax design features one-knob control. The single knob (1) inserts the pricker into the tip (preventing fuel from coming out) and (2) simultaneously turns off a foot-valve located down inside the lantern. If the lantern is out of adjustment, however, and the foot valve is not in synch with the pricker, then fuel will leak out of the tip and the only way to turn the lantern completely off is to release pressure from the font.

But when you release pressure you are not releasing just air from the font. You are also releasing some vaporized fuel; you can smell it. Releasing pressure during a flare-up means a bit of vaporized fuel is wafting about in the vicinity of an open flame. And that can result in a 'flashback.' What part of *fun* don't you understand?

Okay, enough on preheating for the moment. To avoid getting too far ahead of ourselves, let's swing over to a discussion of Coleman kerosene models. We'll bring preheating (and safety concerns) back into the conversation as appropriate.

COLEMAN KEROSENE LANTERNS

Here's where the rubber meets the road. Although, as a fuel, kerosene is widely available, kerosene pressure lanterns are not. In September 2011 there were 428 Coleman pressure lanterns for sale on eBay. I counted them. *Ten* were kerosene; 418 were gas. So in the Coleman universe, even a 'common' kerosene model is rare.

Model 247

■ **ABOVE:** *The Coleman Model 247 is rated as 300 CP. It's a single-mantle lantern. It replaced the 242K in 1937 so it predates World War II. Its predecessor, the 242K, had a straight-sided globe; the 247 has a bulge-globe. The 247 had two color schemes: (1) a green font and green ventilator, or (2) a nickel-plated font and green ventilator.* ■

Some 247's have the word 'Scout' embossed on the collar although I'm not aware of any connection between the '247 Scout' and the 'Boy Scouts of America.' The 247 Scouts have the generator size (TK66) printed on the bottom in black ink.

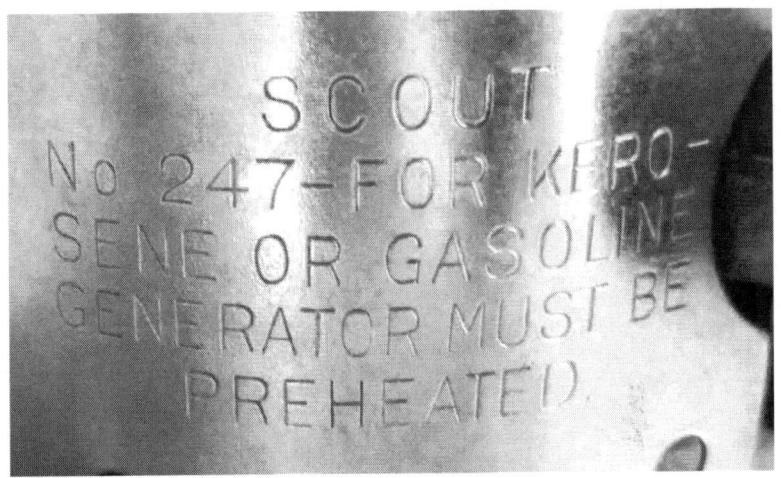

■ **ABOVE:** *The collar on the Coleman 247 Scout says, "For kerosene or gasoline generator must be preheated." The 'gasoline' in question is white gas (Coleman fuel). In an era where Coleman Instant-Lite lamps were common (and the Instant-Lite claim to fame was that it did not require preheating), this stamped-in message was a reminder that the 247 was NOT an Instant-Lite and that it DID require preheating. Failure to preheat the 247 would have produced a flare-up when you attempted to light it.* ■

Please refer to *Book 5: Coleman Gas Lanterns* for an explanation of Instant-Lite lanterns and their predecessors, Quick-Lites.

Non-scout 247's (for lack of a better term) have '247 USE GENERATOR №. TK-66' stamped into the collar.

A third variation of the 247 has "C.P.R." embossed in the font and "247 USE GENERATOR №. TK-66" stamped into the collar. C.P.R. stands for Canadian Pacific Railroad. The C.P.R. font is bigger than 'civilian' 247's.

The TK66 generator (no longer made) had a .006" tip. The generator from a Coleman Model 201 (kerosene) lantern can be substituted for a TK66. The 201 generator has a .006" tip.

As regards mantles, a 247 lantern runs best on a Coleman Silk-Lite No. 21A mantle.

About 1949, the (kerosene) Model 247 was superseded with the (kerosene) Model 249. Just like the 247, some 249's have 'Scout' embossed on the collar. The word 'Scout' makes for confusion between the 247 and the 249.

Also, just like the 247, there is no connection I know of between the '249 Scout' and the 'Boy Scouts of America.' The non-scout 249's were made for export, primarily to the Philippines, and are rare in the USA.

The 249's biggest problem is its generator; it is large in diameter (.375") making it unique. There's no substitute available. A key objective of this book is practical day-to-day lighting. A rare generator mounted on a rare lantern translates into skipping over the 249. Although the 247 may be a viable kerosene option, the 249 is not.

Model 201

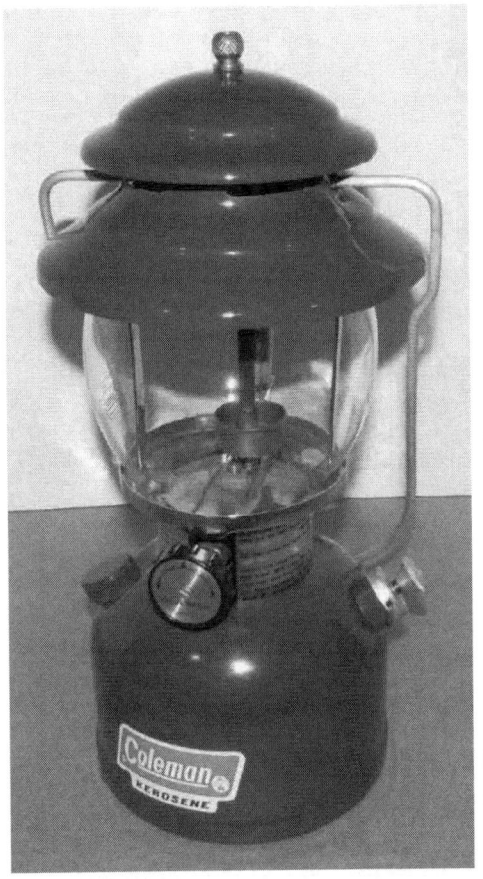

■ **ABOVE:** *The Coleman Model 201 was manufactured from 1974 to 1983. It's a kerosene lantern, rated as 300 CP.* ■

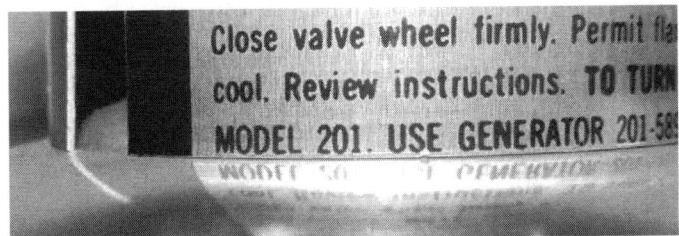

■ **ABOVE:** *The 201 model number is printed (rather than embossed) on the collar. Model 201-700 has a green ventilator and a green font. Model 201-720 has a green ventilator and a nickel-plated font.* ■

■ **ABOVE:** *The 201 was made for the Israeli Defense Force but was also sold to civilians. I've seen the mark shown above on a few eBay 201's, sometimes on the side of the font, sometimes on the bottom. According to the Terrence Marsh Web page, this symbol is the first letter for the word 'army' in Hebrew. (http://tgmarsh.faculty.noctrl.edu/coleuslant6180.htm* ■

Coleman still stocks parts for the 201. And that's a good thing because many conversions (from a gas lantern to kero) require a 201 generator.

Now, what mantle should we use on the 201?

The short answer is this. The 201 was designed for a Silk-Lite No. 21A mantle and that original mantle, as you might expect, works great. However, a #21 mantle (what Walmart sells today) also works great.

Here's the long version . . .

The printed 201 lantern directions call for a 21A3101 mantle. In olden days, the advertising on the mantle package said "Silk-Lite No. 21A" and the small print said

"21A3101" (exactly what the directions called for). But Silk-Lite mantles were thorium (radioactive) and have been discontinued.

Today, the advertising on the mantle package says "#21" and the small print says either "21A102" or "21A104." The numeral '2' at the end indicates a 2-pak; the numeral '4' indicates a 4-pak. The '21A' at the beginning of the small-print number has nothing whatsoever to do with the Silk-Lite 21A. Its only apparent function is to confuse customers. Call it a Coleman thing.

The modern-day #21 mantle is yttrium and non-radioactive. This lantern, the Coleman 201, will run kerosene on a modern-day #21 mantle, no problem.

On the downside, the 201 will not burn diesel fuel. Not with a #21 mantle nor with a Silk-Lite No. 21A mantle. After a couple of minutes on diesel the 201 flares up.

Model 214

■ **ABOVE:** *The Coleman Model 214 was rated by Coleman as 200 CP. It was produced from 1985 to 2010 or thereabouts. The 214 has only one control knob. The pricker and shutoff valve are joined at the hip, the same as the 639C, discussed below.* ■

The 214 has a big brother, the 639C. The printed directions that come with the 214 specify a '21A' mantle. The 639C directions specify a '1111' mantle. Those are clearly Silk-Lite numbers although the word 'Silk-Lite' is never never never never never used.

Because of the radioactivity issue (in the politically correct 1980's), thorium Silk-Lite No. 21A's and thorium Silk-Lite No. 1111's were *out.* Yttrium #21's and yttrium #11's were *in.* Almost.

About the time the Model 214 kerosene lantern was being introduced, Coleman came out with 'Gold Top' mantles. (And the mantle tops were indeed yellow; today's mantles have green tops.)

Gold Tops were Coleman's first venture into yttrium mantles. Gold Tops turned out to be an interim product. They were made in every size. The '21' size Gold Top was numbered '21A309G.' Probably 'G' stands for gold top.

Gold Tops were later discontinued. What had been the Silk-Lite No. 21A was replaced with the (green top) #21. If you go on-line to Coleman's official parts list for the Model 214, what they are selling as mantles for the 214 are #21's. But the directions that came with the lantern were never changed; the directions always specified the '21A' as the mantle to use.
http://www.coleman.com/Parts/RNRP/repair-replacement-parts/214-700/1-mantle-kerosene-lantern

That clears things up, eh?

The 214 has a reputation for running a yellow flame and/or flaring up. That's a clear indication the generator is not hot enough. Eliminating #21 mantles and resorting to old-time Silk-Lite No. 21A mantles would likely solve the problem. Old-time thorium Silk-Lites burn hotter than new-generation yttrium mantles.

Using an 'Amish mix' of 30% white gas and 70% kero (rather than 100% kero) would likely solve the problem. The Amish mix would have a lower flash point and vaporize more easily than pure kero.

33

Doing both things simultaneously (Amish mix plus Silk-Lite mantles) would almost certainly solve the problem.

Actually, I must confess, I've never had the problem. My 214 runs just fine on 100% kero plus a #21 yttrium mantle. Then again, I've learned to be careful about preheating.

The 214 will not run diesel, even with a Silk-Lite No. 21A thorium mantle.

Plastic. This is a troublesome topic for me. The 214 was introduced in an era when, for cost-saving purposes, plastic parts were being substituted for metal parts throughout American industry. I remember having a Plymouth car in which the water pump broke. It was a simple plastic impellor fastened to a shaft with what resembled gear teeth (*plastic* gear teeth). The gear teeth had all sheared off. The replacement part from the auto parts store was a metal impellor with metal gear teeth.

A lifetime of similar experiences has frankly prejudiced me against plastic. The 214's 'valve assembly' (Part 214A5571) has what looks to be a plastic fuel pick-up tube that goes down into the font. It's pictured here: http://www.ereplacementparts.com/valve-assy-p-1003452.html

Is that a deal-breaker? Or is it harmless? Your call.

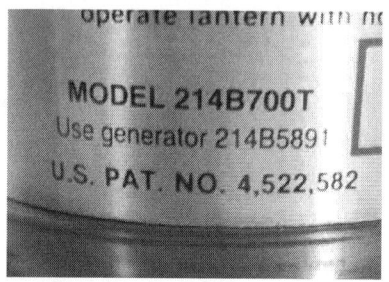

■ **ABOVE:** *The 214 Model number is printed on the collar.* ■

Model 237

■ **ABOVE:** *The 237 was made from 1940 to 1974. It's a single-mantle kerosene lantern, designed for the big Coleman Silk-Lite No. 1111 mantle. It runs fine in today's Coleman #11 mantle. The 237 is rated as 500 CP.* ■

Many consider the 237 to be the best kerosene pressure lantern ever made. For sure it carries a premium price.

There is an on-line organization called *The International Guild of Lamp Researchers* (http://www.lampguild.org/). The Guild archives contain a couple of million words (literally) on lamping issues of all sorts. Neal McRae (a Brit but we won't hold that against him) is one of the founding Guild members and as well as one of its chief authorities.

Per *Guild Question #3015*, McRae writes: "My recommendation for a kero lamp that can run on gasoline if need be is always Coleman 237 . . . [It's] my preferred lantern when out camping . . . and I have over 300 [lanterns] to choose from . . . the light output is stunning."

■ **ABOVE:** *The 237 'Empire' was made in Canada. There was also a 237 and 237A. I'm not sure what the differences were between the 237, the 237A, and the Empire. The Canadian Empire had a companion gasoline model, the 236, called the 'Major.'* ■

■ **ABOVE:** *In the 237 world, this ventilator is above average.* ■

Unfortunately, 237 ventilators are invariably in bad shape. They are too well-made; too sturdy; too thick; too heavy. They have no flex. The vitreous enamel (glass beads or 'frits' melted and bonded to steel) cracks easily, both from expansion/contraction (due to heat) as well as rolling around in the back of Buba's pickup truck. An ugly ventilator does not impair light output but sure looks crappy. A cosmetically pretty ventilator will double the price of a 237.

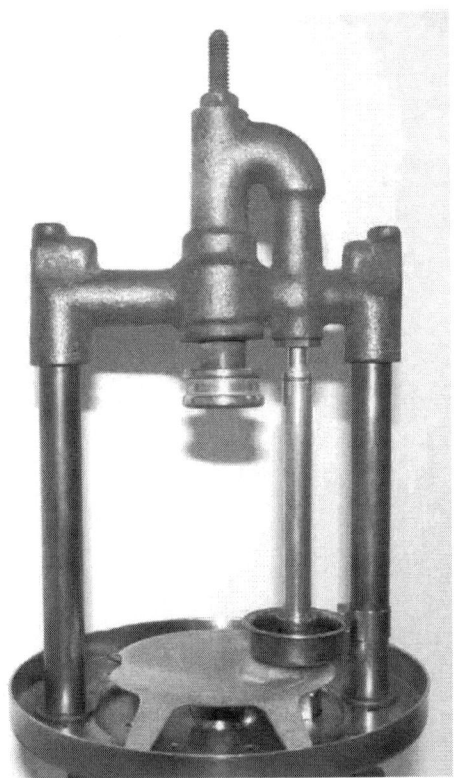

■ **ABOVE:** *A lot of bronze castings here. The 237 without bail, ventilator, or globe weighs in at 3 lb. 10 oz. It really is quite a lantern.* ■

Model 639

■ **ABOVE:** *The 237 was replaced by the 639, also rated as 500 CP. Shown here is the original 639 with a fuel shutoff knob on the right and a separate cleaning lever (pricker) on the left. To avoid any ambiguity or confusion, I'm going to call this the 639-with-pricker. In newer lanterns – the 639B and 639C – there is only one knob; the pricker and shutoff valve are joined at the hip. We'll get to those in a moment.* ■

When in production, the 639-with-pricker was never as popular as the 237 it replaced. Nor was it made for as many years. So today it is fairly rare. On eBay a 639-with-pricker sells for double the price of a Model 237 in comparable condition.

Ironically, although designed to be cheap (to save on material costs I'm sure), the 639-with-pricker turns out to be King of the Road as far as multi-fuel lanterns are concerned. The 639 manifold has a large surface area to absorb heat. A 639-with-pricker, fitted with nothing more exotic than today's Coleman #11 yttrium mantle, will burn white gas, mineral spirits, kerosene, and diesel. All on the same stock 639 generator.

From gas to diesel on the same lantern? Same generator? Same yttrium mantle? This is the Law of Unintended Consequences in action. I seriously doubt Coleman ever intended to gift the world with such an item.

■ **ABOVE:** *The model number for the 639-with-pricker was embossed on the lamp's collar. The 639-with-pricker had two color schemes: (1) a green font and green ventilator, and (2) a nickel-plated font and green ventilator.* ■

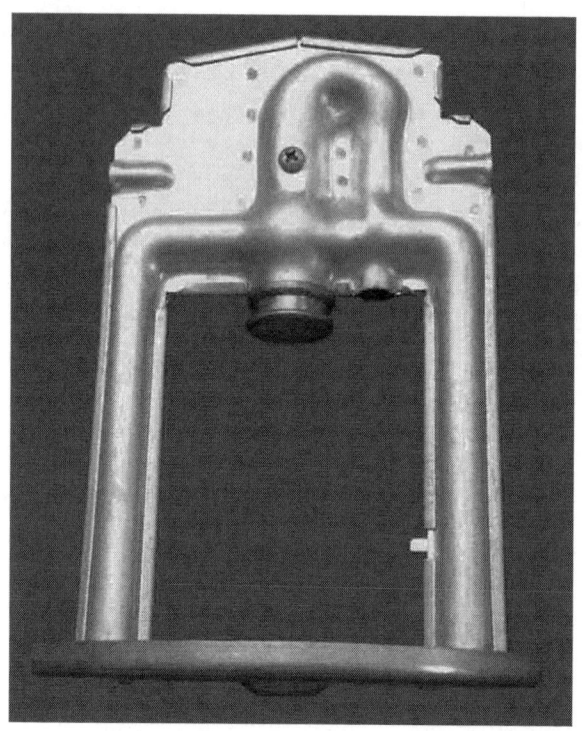

■ **ABOVE:** *For sure the 639-with-pricker was cheaper to produce than the 237 it replaced. The 639 manifold is a sandwich of rolled, folded, and spot welded steel. (Check it out with a magnet.) Without a bail, ventilator, or globe, a 639-with-pricker weighs in at 2 lb. 11 oz.* ■

Side note. The 639-with-pricker was designed and sold as a kerosene lantern. In *Guild Question #3015,* Neil McRae explicitly states that the Coleman 639 is safe on gasoline.

Model 639C

■ **ABOVE:** *The 639C, Coleman's latest-and-greatest, currently in production. In fact, it's the only kerosene lantern Coleman is currently producing [in 2015]. The 639C has a pricker, but it and the fuel shutoff valve are joined at the hip; there is no separate cleaning lever/pricker. The 639C is advertised as producing 784 lumens.* ■

There's a mini-mystery about the 639B/C (at least to me). If you go to Coleman's on-line parts page, you'll find the 'B' model listed, not the 'C' model. But if you buy a 'B' model lantern on-line, what arrives in the box will be a 'C'.

Throughout this book I've used the 'C' suffix because I've never seen a 'B' in real life. And I've even read reference to a 639A. (Do A's and B's really exist? Well . . .)

The 639C (like the 214 mentioned earlier) does not have a pricker separate from the fuel shutoff. To my mind, that makes it similar to a Petromax wherein a single knob simultaneously controls the pricker as well as a foot-valve down inside the lantern. The same knob controls *liquid* fuel going font-to-generator AND *vaporized* fuel going generator-to-mantle.

I'm sure you could argue about the safety merits all day. But please know that, performance-wise, the 639C lights easily, no fuss, no muss. And, per the directions, you can adjust light output with the control knob.

On the downside, the 639C will not burn diesel. Don't even think about it. And there's the same plastic issue we discussed above in regard to the Model 214. On the 'Old Coleman Parts' web page the 'fuel air tube' for the 639C (SKU 639-5231) is pictured and looks to be plastic. http://www.oldcolemanparts.com/product.php?productid=6 55

CONVERSIONS

Our options for obtaining a kerosene pressure lantern are (1) a Coleman designed for kerosene, (2) a Petromax, and (3) a Coleman gas-to-kerosene conversion.

We just described Coleman lanterns designed specifically for kerosene (247, 201, 214, 237, 639-with-pricker, and 639C). None of these six are truly 'rare' but neither are they common. There are several hundred Coleman gas lanterns on eBay at any given time but only a dozen or so Coleman kerosene lanterns.

Our second option, Petromax, is of German origin and was designed for kerosene. There are always a bunch on eBay, both new and used. But the Petromax has its own issues. You really should brush up on it before jumping in.

Our third option is to convert a Coleman gas lantern to run on kerosene. And that's not as farfetched as it may sound. Cost-wise, a conversion might well be your biggest bang for the buck. Coleman itself once made lamps and lanterns that ran on either fuel, gas or kerosene.

On the topic of conversions, incidentally, it needs to be mentioned that you can't run a given lantern-mantle-generator combo for 20 minutes on kerosene and declare success. I've had pressure lamps run smoothly on kerosene for well over an hour and then flare up or carbon up.

So my criterion is to let something run for *two hours minimum* before declaring victory. By simple trial and error, I've found that if something runs on kerosene for two hours without incident then you can expect it to run forever without incident. Well, maybe not *forever*. That's a long time.

Are Conversions Safe?

Without a doubt, Coleman gas lanterns can be altered (by changing the generator) to modify the fuel/oxygen ratio and burn kerosene. But is it safe to do so?

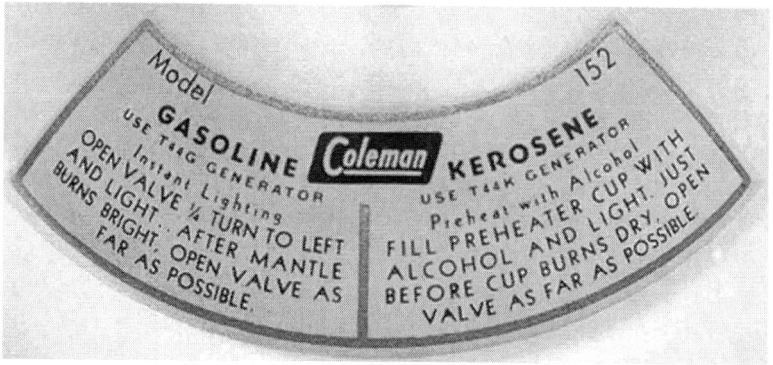

Please examine the illustrations above. Clearly, a Coleman gas lantern can be modified to burn kerosene. But is it a safe?

Answer. Coleman always thought so.

What's a 'Full Conversion'?

Question. On eBay, I've seen Coleman Model 200's advertised as being 'fully converted' to kerosene. What's that all about?

Answer. The Model 200 is an Instant-Lite. To facilitate lighting, an Instant-Lite uses a special fuel-air tube.

In round numbers, here's how the 'Instant-Lite' feature works. A 'fuel-and-air' pickup tube runs from the generator down to the bottom of the fuel tank. The tube has two holes: one near the bottom of the tank to pick up fuel and a second hole, higher up, in the air space above the fuel, to pick up air.

After pumping in pressure, turning the fuel valve ¼ turn opens both holes. A mixture of fuel and air travels up to the mantle where it's lit with a match, burns with a relatively low flame, and preheats the generator. Of course it's consuming air pressure out of the tank while it does this.

Once the lantern has preheated itself and the "mantle burns bright," the valve is turned full open. Doing so turns off the upper hole and no additional combustion air comes from inside the tank; all combustion air then comes from outside the lantern. Pressure then needs to be pumped back into the tank to replace the air consumed during preheat.

My gas-to-kero conversions outlined below all leave the fuel-air tube undisturbed. Some folks think that replacing the Instant-Lite fuel-air tube with a simple fuel tube creates a more authentic kerosene lantern and they term it a 'full conversion.'

But please consider the pictures above. Both the Coleman 139 and the Coleman 152 (when operating in gas mode) are Instant-Lites. The gas lighting instructions are clearly Instant-Lite instructions.

As designed by Coleman, only a generator change is required to convert the 139 or the 152 from gas to kerosene. Obtaining the appropriate fuel-to-oxygen ratio can be accomplished with the generator alone. There's no need to mess around with the fuel-air tube down inside the tank. At least that's what Coleman thought.

Coleman 285 Conversion

First up for conversion is the Coleman 285 Dual Fuel. It's the least expensive of Coleman's present-day 285-286-288-290-295 lineup.

The 285 caused me to change my thinking about what could be converted from gas to kero. It even caused me to go back and retest earlier conclusions.

I've seen it claimed that you can add a preheater cup to a stock 285 Dual Fuel and burn kerosene. (http://www.youtube.com/watch?v=b4gc7TP-4M4)

It didn't work for me. I tried it with different lanterns and different mantles and it didn't work. All I ever got was flare-ups.

I've also seen it claimed that mounting a 214 (kerosene) generator on a 285 will convert the 285 into a kerosene-burning lantern.
www.ar15.com/archive/topic.html?b=10&f=18&t=643799

That, too, never worked for me. The best result I ever achieved was to get the lantern running at a 50-watt level. Then, after an hour, the mantles (#21) carboned up. Silk-Lite No. 21A mantles did not cure the problem. It simply did not work.

Then came a breakthrough.

Prepper4u, a poster on YouTube, demonstrated lighting a Coleman 285 filled with kerosene. He did it by removing the ventilator and glass globe and preheating the generator for *two minutes* with a propane torch. And it worked, at least in his demo. So I tried it. And *it worked*. Hat tip to Prepper4u!

Big change to my thinking, to my phenomenological field.

You see, I had always preheated a Coleman kerosene lantern with a preheater cup of alcohol. That's the way preheating is done, yes? But with some lanterns *that's not enough heat*.

The 285 experience made me realize that a hierarchy of preheating exists.

First, which alcohol (methanol, ethanol, denatured, or isopropyl) gives the most heat? Second, some kerosene lanterns won't start properly on one cup-worth of alcohol. But they'll run just fine given two cups.

CAUTION: If you use two preheater cups of alcohol, one after the other, be careful. When filling the second cup, it may just take fire all by itself; call it 'spontaneous ignition.' If that happens, *stop!* Simply allow whatever amount of alcohol you managed to get in the cup to burn down. If you add alcohol to an already burning cup, the small fill-flask in your hand will catch fire. If in haste you fumble and spill some alcohol down into the lantern you may well get a POP that shreds your mantles into a thousand pieces. Just sayin'.

Third, some lanterns that won't run using preheater cups will run using a propane torch. (At two minutes with a propane torch, the brass generator glows a dull red. You can see it in dim light. So please keep the torch moving if you use this method; don't dwell in one spot; don't risk melting a hole in the generator.)

The 285 experience made me realize that, if there was a lantern that was *almost* able to run kerosene with a preheat cup, then torch preheating might push it over the edge and make it happen.

Likewise for diesel. If there was a lantern that was *almost* able to run diesel, then torch preheating might make it happen. Torch preheating thus threw into question some of the conclusions I'd drawn from previous lantern-fuel-generator-mantle combinations.

Back to the drawing board.

■ **ABOVE:** *The Coleman 285 Dual Fuel will run kerosene (smoothly; without pulsing) if equipped with a 214 generator and*

preheated two minutes with a propane torch. (But it will not run on diesel.) ∎

The 285 Dual Fuel is considered the gas twin of the 214 kerosene lantern. The 285 is advertised as running on either white gas (Coleman fuel) or automobile gas. But I've found that the factory-issue 285 generator gradually plugs on auto gas. Seventeen hours was the most I ever got on auto gas before the 285 was dead in the water.

And using kerosene for a fuel certainly doesn't help the plugging situation. Based on several experiments, I would expect the 285 generator (with filter) to clog on kerosene before the 50-hour mark. (Fifty hours is an upper limit; problems within 15 to 20 hours are far more likely.)

If you need to run your lantern an evening or two on kerosene to get through a rough patch, of course, the stock 285 generator (with a filter inside) should do the job. But, to run kerosene long-term, you need a 214 generator (designed for the Coleman 214 kerosene lantern). The 214 generator does not have a filter.

Preheating Revisited

Because of my 285 experience, and because lanterns flare up if not properly preheated, we need to consider preheating in more detail. First, which of the available alcohols give the best preheat results?

● *Methanol* is 'wood alcohol' and is poisonous. 'Heet' is a brand-name of methanol, used to start cars in the winter.

● *Ethanol* is 'grain alcohol' and is drinkable. But drinkable means taxable and taxable means expensive. So I'm going to ignore ethanol and pretend that it's not even on the list.

• *Denatured alcohol* is ethanol with some methanol added (making it poisonous, undrinkable, nontaxable, and cheap). Denatured alcohol is sold by the gallon in hardware stores. It's used as fuel in marine stoves.

• *Isopropyl* (also non-drinkable) is rubbing alcohol. Most isopropyl is 70% alcohol (30% water) but 91% isopropyl (9% water) is also available at drugstores and even Walmart.

I tested the three alcohols *ceteris paribus* (all else being equal). The methanol and denatured alcohol each took 6 minutes 45 seconds (405 seconds total) to boil water. The 91% isopropyl took 7 minutes 15 seconds (435 seconds total). The isopropyl thus took 7% longer than the other two.

Second, torches. Here are three torches you can use for 'torch preheating':

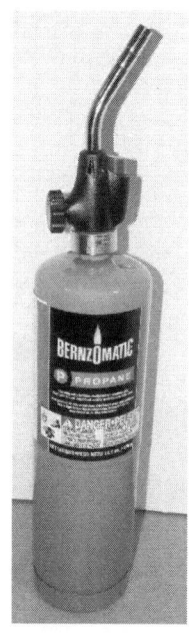

■ **ABOVE:** *A propane torch. The cost is about $15. On the upside, propane torches and replacement propane fuel cylinders are widely available. On the downside, a propane torch is comparatively big and clumsy. OK at home. Not so great for backpacking.* ■

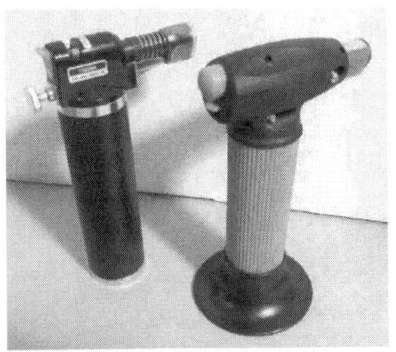

■ **ABOVE:** *Refillable butane torches. The one on the left is good quality and costs about $25. The one on the right is a cheapie. It only costs $6 but it leaks. Put in butane tonight and tomorrow morning it will be empty.* ■

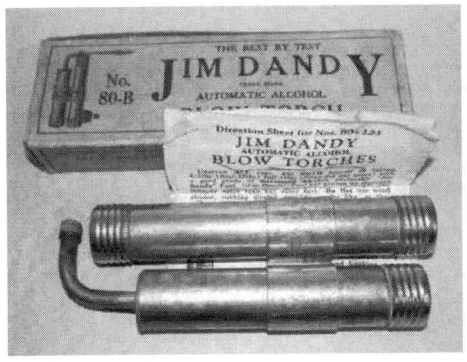

■ **ABOVE:** *The Jim Dandy (brand) alcohol blow torch comes from the World War II era. It's available (used) on eBay for about $25. Get one that includes directions because how to use this device is not intuitively obvious. The fuel is denatured alcohol. Mechanically, the Jim Dandy works fine; it lost out in the marketplace due to the convenience of propane and butane torches. (This is not unlike Coleman liquid-fuel lanterns losing market share to propane lanterns. Convenience sells.)* ■

Coleman 200A Conversion

■ **ABOVE:** *The Instant-Lite 200A was produced 1952-1983. It had one mantle and was rated as 300 candlepower.* ■

In November 2012 I put out an 11-minute YouTube video demonstrating the conversion of a 200A to kerosene: (https://www.youtube.com/watch?v=ifpvKE-2Uxk).

I chose the 200A because it's the simplest and most straightforward conversion. Also, the 200A itself is very common. There are 120 for sale on eBay as we speak.

Coleman Models 220 and/or 228 were Coleman's most popular gas lanterns. But they require two mantles. For the prepper, given a choice, the 200A (with one mantle) makes more sense.

Mantles are the Achilles' heel of pressure lanterns. Mantles are fragile. They do not take well to the vibration of automobile transportation, for example. When you get down to your last couple of spare mantles, do you want, at that point, a lantern that can run on ONE mantle? Or a lantern that demands TWO?

The 200A is considered the gas twin of the kerosene 201 lantern. A 201 generator fits the 200A perfectly. To convert the 200A to kerosene, you need only three things: (1) a 201 generator, (2) a preheater cup, and (3) a Silk-Lite No. 21A mantle. This setup will not run kerosene using a #21 mantle.

On the YouTube video, referenced above, a couple of viewers asked if the Coleman Model 200 was the same as the 200A and could be converted to kerosene in the same way as the 200A.

My answer was that the Model 200 was made for only one year (1951) and was replaced by the 200A. The limited production makes the Model 200 fairly rare and I never had one to experiment with. Likely the same conversion would work but I can't positively say so.

Coleman 275 Conversion

■ **ABOVE:** *Coleman 275. Produced in the 1970's and 80's. It was designed for white gas (Coleman fuel). It did not have a pricker separate from the fuel shutoff valve. As equipped from the factory, the 275 used a 220 generator. The 275 gained a reputation for occasionally turning into a fireball. Brown in color, matching the coppertone kitchen appliances of the day, it was dubbed 'the Coleman turd.'* ■

The conversion of a 275 to kerosene is identical to the conversion of a 200A: a 201 generator, a preheater cup, and Silk-Lite No. 21A mantles.

Although the conversion steps are the same, the results are not. The hole in the air tube of the 275 is designed to accept the bigger 220 generator. So extra air is being sucked into the mixing chamber around the edges of the 201 generator. Consequently, the 275 (running on kerosene with a 201 generator) makes what I'd call a 'fluttering' sound (not quite the same as the 'ragged' noise many other lanterns make as they burn).

But the 275 does not pulse or 'hunt' on kerosene. The conversion is a wee bit noisy but gives a steady 200 watts-worth of white light and has no filter to plug. What's not to like?

Coleman 242 Conversion

■ **ABOVE:** *In looks, except for the writing on the collar, the 242 is identical to its kerosene twin, the 247 (q.v.).* ■

What I've found sprinkled about on-line is this. The 242A was made 1935-36. The 242B was made 1937-42. The 242C was made 1942-50. The 242 made for export was numbered 246.

To burn kerosene in a 242, you need a 201 generator, a preheater cup, and a Silk-Lite No. 21A mantle.

■ **ABOVE:** *The 242 is an Instant-Lite gas lantern but the directions are printed on the collar, not on the knob.* ■

Coleman 220 & 228 Conversion

HOW TO USE and ENJOY YOUR NEW...

Coleman® **220F & 228F LANTERN**

■ **ABOVE:** *The 220 and 228 even shared the same instruction manual. Both use a 220 generator. The 228 cost a few dollars more and so was less common.* ■

■ **ABOVE:** *This is the Coleman Instant-Lite 220, introduced in 1944. There were several models (220C through 220K and maybe more), sold into the 1980's. They were designed for white gas (Coleman fuel). The 220's had two mantles. They were rated at 300 candlepower. This is the lantern that everybody had with their camping gear after World War II. There are still a lot of them around. There are over 300 for sale on eBay as we speak.* ■

I spent a fair amount of time testing and puzzling over the conversion of a 220 and/or 228 to kerosene. "Why bother?" you ask. "What's so special about the 220/228?"

Well, let's say you search eBay for other Coleman models. You'll find maybe ten Model 285's for sale. And Coleman

237's? Three. And Coleman 639C's? Six. If you look up every Coleman model number you can think of (200A, 201, 242, 247, 214, 635, 639, 286, 288, 290, 295, 275, 335, 339, 236, etc.) and add them all together, you'll find, in total, about 150 lanterns for sale.

But there are *three hundred* Model 220/228's for sale on eBay right now, double the number of all other liquid-fuel Coleman models combined. That makes Coleman 220's and 228's the least expensive lanterns available. That's where you'll find the bargains.

■ **ABOVE:** *The Coleman 220 had a fraternal twin, the Coleman 228. The only difference between the two was the ventilator or 'hat' size. The 228 hat was 8.5" in diameter whereas the 220 was 7". All else was the same.* ■

My test results showed that, on the 220/228, the best generator for kerosene was a 220 barrel and everything else from a 201: tip, pricker, and spring. To be clear, the 201 spring (one piece) replaces the 220 filter-and-spring (two pieces). The best mantle was a Coleman Silk-Lite No. 21A. One preheater cup of alcohol was sufficient on both kerosene and diesel.

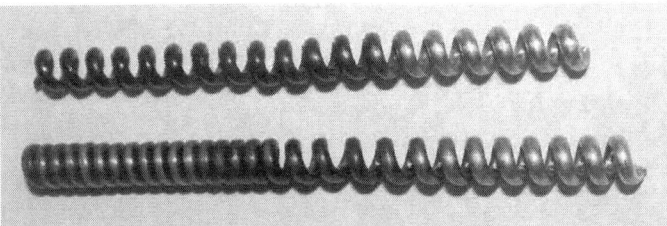

■ **ABOVE:** *When you buy a 201 generator, it may come with either of two springs inside. Here, the one pictured on top is the spring you want. It comes inside the 201A5891 generator. The spring pictured on the bottom is the one you don't want. You cannot burn kerosene or diesel in a 220 with this spring; it comes inside the 201B5891 generator. (Note. The springs pictured here are blackish on one end because they have been used.)* ■

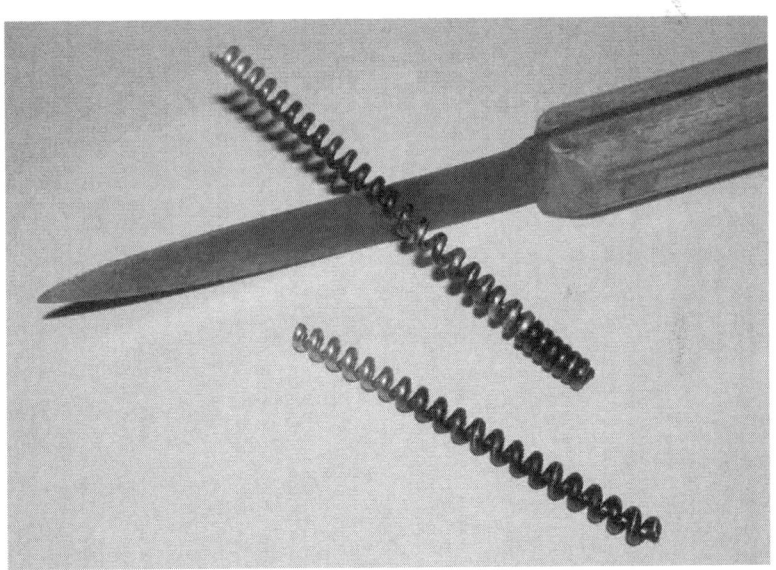

■ **ABOVE:** *The lower spring (the one you want) is 2½" long and has 19 evenly-spaced coils or loops. It comes from a 201A generator. Above that is a 201B spring being modified to match the 201A spring.* ■

You can spread out the spacing between the coils of a 201B spring by working it back and forth over the edge of a dull kitchen knife. At the end of the rolling, make a final adjustment by stretching and/or compressing the spring with your fingers. (Although called a 'spring' because of its shape, there is no temper or springiness in the metal; it appears to be aluminum; it does not attract a magnet.) Cut your counterfeit spring to finished length with sidecutters. If your efforts produce a 2½" spring with 19 evenly spaced circlets, it will work.

On kerosene, the converted 220 produces 200+ watts-worth of light with faint pulsing. Some of my test notes say "weak audible and visual pulsing" while other annotations say "faint audible pulsing only." Preheating with a propane torch did not reduce the pulsing.

Pulsing bugs me although I must admit that what I'm complaining about here is pretty feeble. My wife, in fact, tells me I'm imagining things.

Actually, this conversion runs smoother on diesel fuel than it does on kerosene. You can hang a big smiley face on that; burning diesel in a Coleman 220 is a fairly major accomplishment. The only bad news is that I just dislocated my shoulder patting myself on the back.

Coleman 236 Conversion

■ **ABOVE:** *The 236 (Major) is the gas twin of the kerosene 237 (Empire).* ■

The 236 gas generator is smaller in diameter than the 237 kerosene generator. Consequently, the 237 generator cannot be mounted on the 236 lantern.

So I used the barrel from the 236 generator and filled in everything else from a 237: tip, pricker, and small spring.

The gas 236 has a filter and a spring. The kerosene 237 has two springs: a small-diameter inner spring surrounded by a larger spring. I replaced the 236 filter-and-spring with the 237 small-diameter spring (only). There is no room inside the 236 barrel for the larger spring.

Adding a preheater cup and a Silk-Lite No. 1111 mantle created a lantern up in the 500-candlepower range. This combo is a winner. It runs smoothly, no pulsing, on both kerosene and diesel.

Coleman 635 Conversion

I expected great things from the 635. It's the gas twin of the 639-with-pricker (the lantern that will run anything from white gas to diesel on the same generator). The 635 has the same cold-rolled steel manifold as the 639-with-pricker so I was a little disappointed with the 635 results.

Oh well. Like they say, some days you get the bear; some days the bear gets you.

■ **ABOVE:** *This is a variation of the 635. It's a 635B721, made by Coleman for the Leacock Coleman Center in Ronks, PA. A unique feature of the Leacock 635B is that the 'cleaning lever' must be in the UP position for the lantern to operate, opposite any other Coleman I've ever seen.* ■

Made by
The Coleman Company
for Leacock Coleman Center
Ronks, PA 17572-0307

Model 635B721
Uses Generator 635-589
Uses Mantle 1111

■ **ABOVE:** *The model number is printed (rather than embossed) on the collar.* ■

The 635 and the Leacock 635B delivered the same performance. My best results on both kerosene and diesel came from a Silk-Lite No. 1111 mantle plus a 639 generator (.009" tip). Kerosene ran with a slight pulsing. With diesel the pulsing was a bit stronger.

Was it real bad? No. You could certainly use it out in the shop to fix the car. You could certainly use it in an emergency to deliver a baby. Or in a non-emergency to cook supper. But it's not something I'd want to use every night to read the Bible. After a few minutes of squinting and squirming I would no doubt start yelling blasphemous things. Praise the Lord.

Coleman 335 Conversion

■ **ABOVE:** *The 335 is an Instant-Lite gas lantern from the 1970's rated at 350CP. The globe on the 335 has straight sides, not bulged. It was produced in an all-red version, an all-green version, and as a green Sport-lite model.* ■

Like the 665 and the 639, the Coleman 335 has a cold-rolled steel manifold. Its generator, however, is quite a bit shorter in length than the 639. The Coleman 335 is the gas twin of the (kerosene) Coleman 339.

Wait a minute. Hold on. Forgive me but after a while these numbers all start to blur together: 665 – 335 – 639 – 339. You mean it was somebody's *job* to come up with Coleman model numbers? Somebody's *career*? Somebody with a corner office? And he got a Christmas bonus besides? Gimme a break! Merciful #@$%\## heavens!

OK. Rant over. If the 335 is equipped with a preheater cup and a 339 kerosene generator (.006" tip) it will burn *kerosene* using a #21 mantle (smoothly; no pulsing). It will burn *diesel* using a Silk-Lite No. 21A mantle (likewise smoothly; no pulsing).

Unfortunately the kerosene 339 is rare and so are the 339 generators. At least that's what the books say. In real life I have several times found 339 generators on eBay.

Leacock Model 107 Conversion

You can buy the Model 107 from the Leacock Coleman Center in Ronks, PA:
http://www.leacockcolemancenter.com/Stainless-Steel-Table-Lamp-Leacock-Lamp-107SS/item/107SS

■ **ABOVE:** *The Leacock Model 107. It features a stainless steel font.* ■

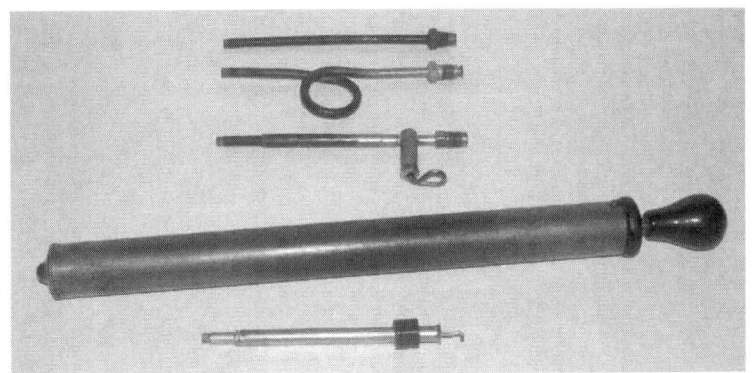

■ **ABOVE:** *The Model 107 resembles a Coleman 1920's Quick-Lite table lamp. But the three Quick-Lite generators shown here at the top (a Q77, Q99, and R55) all have male 'jam nuts' on the right end and will not fit the modern-day Model 107. The 220 generator at the bottom (used by the Model 107) employs a 'flare nut.' The second item up from the bottom is an external pump. The pump can be used on either an old-time Quick-Lite or a brand new Model 107.* ■

The Model 107 conversion to kerosene is easy. Replace the spring-and-filter inside its 220 generator with a spring (only) from a Coleman 214 (kerosene) generator. Keep all the other 220-generator components 'as is' including the .008" tip.

Given this generator modification (and removing the air-tube choke collar, explained below) the Model 107 operates perfectly on kerosene using #21 mantles. That, in itself is remarkable. A preheater cup, of course, must be mounted on the generator and the lamp preheated with a cup of alcohol at startup. Light output on kerosene is over 200 watts.

The Model 107 is pricey. The lamp itself (no shade) is $175. The other stuff you can get on eBay. Glass shade ($50) plus pump ($15) plus 214 generator ($10) plus preheater cup ($3). Plus postage all 'round.

But you'll have a brand new stainless steel font that's not old and dented and shedding rust particles (like me). And you don't have to wait for it to appear on eBay. And it runs beautifully on both white gas and kerosene – *la crème-de-la-crème* of dual-fuel lamps.

■ **ABOVE:** *The bottom of the air intake tube is threaded. The lamp comes from the factory with a choke collar mounted on the air intake, providing the correct amount of air to burn gas.* ■

■ **ABOVE:** *The choke collar. The hole ID is ⁹/₃₂".* ■

■ **ABOVE:** *With the choke collar removed, the hole in the air intake tube is increased to $^{13}/_{32}$" in diameter. If I did my arithmetic correctly, the air supply is more than doubled by removing the collar.* ■

I did my best to get the Model 107 to run on diesel.

I tried three different mantles (#21, Silk-Lite No. 21A, and Silk-Lite No. 1111) and three different tips (220/.008; 200A/.007; 201/.006) and three different preheat methods and two different mixtures of springs and things inside the generator. If you're into combinations and permutations, it was a long day.

Bottom line. No can do.

DIESEL FUEL

Diesel is widely available and thus a great alternative fuel. Potentially. To my knowledge, there are no lanterns designed specifically for it. If a Coleman model *does* happen to run on diesel, it's more of a fluke than anything else. (But it sure would be nice if we could identify those flukes, no?)

- **639-with-pricker.** From a cost point of view, the 639-with-pricker should be last. On eBay, a 639-with-pricker is double the price of a 237 (given comparable quality). But the 639-with-pricker will run diesel on Coleman yttrium #11 mantles. That's its redeeming quality. Every other Coleman on this list requires a Silk-Lite thorium mantle to run diesel. *Please note that the new 639C model (the only kerosene lantern Coleman currently produces) will not run on diesel at all.*

- **Coleman 220 & 228.** Models 220 and/or 228 are the least expensive pressure lanterns available (because they are so plentiful) AND they burn diesel without pulsing. To do so they require Silk-Lite No. 21A mantles, a preheater cup, and a hybrid generator (220 barrel with the tip, pricker, and spring from a 201A5891 generator).

- **Coleman 247 & 242.** The 247 is a kerosene lantern. The 242 is the Instant-Lite gas twin of the 247. Both of these models (given a 201 generator, preheater cup, and a Silk-Lite No. 21A mantle) will burn diesel. There are always some 247's and/or 242's for sale on eBay. Just be careful. Buy them only where you can return them for a refund (should that prove necessary) and check them over carefully. Every one of them has reached full retirement age; none are younger than 65 years old. After all, how many other household appliances do you own that are still running after 65 years?

- **Coleman 237.** The Coleman 237 is a kerosene lantern, touted by some as the best kerosene lantern ever made. That reputation translates into the 237 selling for a premium on eBay. Price-wise, you'll never find a 'bargain.' The 237 will run on diesel given a thorium Coleman No. 1111 mantle.

- **Coleman 236.** The 236 is the gas twin of the 237. The 236 was never as popular as the 237 so not as many were manufactured; that makes the 236 comparatively rare. In addition, there are collectors who would like to have both the 236 (Major) and 237 (Empire) as a matched set. So, here again, price-wise, you'll never find a bargain. Performance is a different story. The 236 runs great on diesel given a preheater cup, Silk-Lite No. 1111 mantles, and a hybrid generator (236 barrel plus a tip, pricker, and small spring from a 237 generator).

- **Coleman 335.** The 335 is the gas twin of the kerosene 339. The 335 will burn diesel smoothly (no pulsing) given a preheater cup, Silk-Lite No. 21A mantles, and a 339 generator. Unfortunately, although the gas 335 lantern is fairly common, the required 339 generator is not.

- **Coleman 635.** The 635 is the gas twin of the kerosene 639-with-pricker. The 635 (given a preheater cup, Silk-Lite No. 1111 mantles, and a 639 generator) will burn diesel but it's not a smooth performer. It 'hunts' or pulses.

- **Petromax.** Petromax is a different brand of lantern entirely from Coleman. Petromax is next up on the agenda for discussion. A 500CP Petromax (that is, 500 candlepower) will burn diesel on today's Coleman #11 yttrium mantles; no need for Silk-Lite No. 1111's. The smaller Petromax model, 150CP, will burn diesel on today's #21 yttrium mantles; no need for Silk-Lite No. 21A's. So, because of mantle versatility if nothing else, if you want to burn diesel then Petromax is worth taking the time to understand.

COLEMAN WARNING

I've attended enough boardroom meetings in my life to appreciate this wouldn't be the great nation it is without a few 'CYA' (Cover Your Fanny) statements. The following is from Coleman. Well, Coleman's lawyers, actually. The purpose of which is to hold Coleman innocent in the event a Coleman customer colors outside the lines and something goes awry. So please be advised:

"Warning

"Coleman replacement parts are intended for use only on specific Coleman products. Any other use of Coleman replacement parts is strictly prohibited. *Use of Coleman replacement parts on the wrong Coleman product, or for non-approved applications, may cause poor product performance and can cause serious personal injury, property damage or death."* [emphasis theirs]

www.coleman.com/coleman/parts/parts_lantern.asp

PETROMAX

■ **ABOVE:** *A Petromax knockoff; Butterfly brand.* ■

I used to have a friend at work who pulled into the parking lot each day in his clanking Volkswagen diesel. He would get out, shaking his head. "When you go to the dealer, they brag about German engineering. They neglect to mention that it's built in Mexico."

Petromax lanterns are like that.

On older lanterns you'll find, stamped into the metal font under the Petromax logo, "Made in Germany" on the left and "Regd" on the right. "Regd" stands for registered. But no Petromax lanterns have been made in Germany since the 1960's. So many newer lanterns (if they say anything at all) say, under the logo, "Germany" on the left (with no mention of "Made in") and "Regd" on the right.

"Germany . . . Regd" doesn't mean the lantern was made in Germany. It doesn't mean the lantern was *registered* in Germany. It means the Petromax *trademark* was registered in Germany. Sweet.

The glass, etched "Made in Germany," means that the glass was made in Germany (not the whole lantern). My BriteLyt (a Petromax knockoff) came in a cardboard box bearing the sticker "Assembled in China." The cynical side of me, I must confess, wonders if the box was assembled in China and the lantern somewhere else.

Back in college – way, way back – back when my roommate took flying lessons and Pontius was a pilot, some of the guys drove VW Beetles. Remember them? The German Beetle contrasted sharply with USA cars wherein each new calendar year saw new models. A '55 Chevy was a lot different than a '48 Chevy. But the Volkswagen Beetle was the same, year after year. If you needed replacement parts, this year's headlight or brake shoe or windshield was identical to what you'd find on a ten-year-old model.

The same philosophy was used with (German) Petromax lanterns. I should say *is*, not *was*, because Petromax lanterns are still made today, brand new. And all the Petromaxes I have seen, even the knockoffs sold under different brand names (like the Butterfly pictured above), come with an exploded parts diagram with the Preston loop (a.k.a. vegaseroberteil or vaporizer) labeled as part #152. The control knob (a.k.a. griffrad or grip wheel) is #111. The tip (a.k.a. vergaserduse or nipple or spray nozzle) is #50. The verbal description might change but the part number is the same.

Regardless of when the lantern was made, or where it was made, or how it was branded, the parts diagram remains the same with the same numbers, unchanged for 80 years. So fiendishly logical. It's enough to give a Coleman engineer the heebie-jeebies.

How It Works

Here's how it works. Under pressure, liquid fuel moves up from the font through the hollow stem and enters the lower arm of the Preston loop. The loop is heated by the mantle (not shown) and the fuel inside the loop is vaporized. Fuel in the gaseous state exits the top arm of the loop and goes to the tip (seen just above the loop in the photo below).

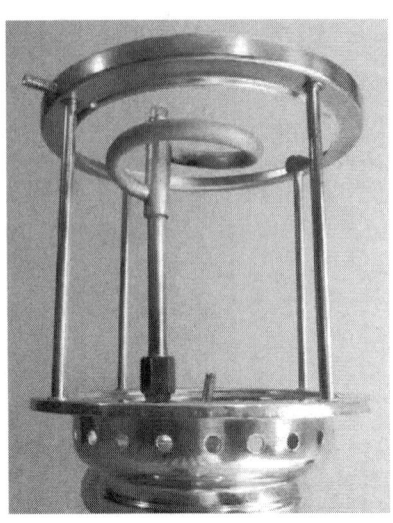

■ **ABOVE:** *Here the Petromax generator-cum-vaporizer-cum-vegaseroberteil-cum-carburettor-cum-Preston loop is shown mounted on the lantern. This helical-coil generator, part #152, is key to the Petromax design.* ■

■ **ABOVE:** *Here we see [A] part #117 (the 'inner cleading' or jacket) holding [B] part #33 (the U-shaped 'mixing shaft') and [C] part #50 (the tip) which is aimed skywards. Fuel in the gaseous state is sprayed upwards from the tip into the mixing shaft. Air is sucked in from the (adjustable) gap between the tip and mixing shaft. The fuel-air mix travels through the mixing shaft and down to the mantle where it burns.* ■

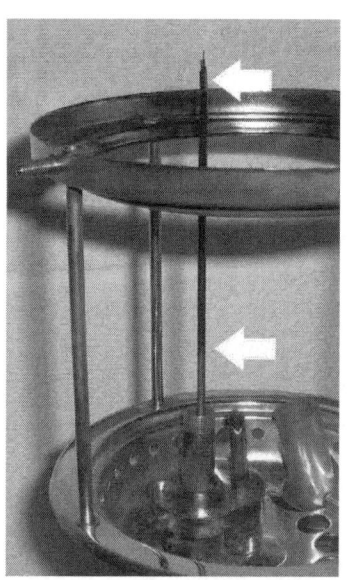

■ **ABOVE:** *Part #101 (the guide rod or führungsstange) typically lives inside the stem of the Preston loop. Here it is shown alone, mounted on the lantern. At the top is a tip-pricker. Down inside the fuel tank is a spring-loaded foot valve that operates in unison with the pricker. Foot valve and pricker (together) turn fuel on. Foot valve and pricker (together) turn fuel off. There's an obstruction inside the stem, between the upper and lower loop-arms, that forces fuel to follow the loop route. The guide rod slides back and forth through a hole in the obstruction.* ■

■ **ABOVE:** *The Preston loop encircles the mantle. It's a robust design. A Petromax burns diesel as readily as kerosene.* ■

Dating a Petromax

Well, the first date is always the most important. Why? Because you never get a second chance to make a first impression. And remember to smile. Wait, wait, wait.

Wrong kind of date, sorry.

The question keeps coming up, "How old is my Petromax?" Fortunately there are ways to approximate a lantern's age and it is sometimes useful to do so (in order to assess parts compatibility, for example).

■ **ABOVE:** *Before 1943 there was an 'E' inside the 'G' on the Erich & Gretz logo. The image on the left shows how it looked printed on the box. The image on the right shows how it looks stamped on the lantern.* ■

■ **ABOVE:** *In 1943 'Erich & Graetz' became 'Graetz AktienGesellschaft Berlin' and the 'E' disappeared from the monogram.* ■

■ **ABOVE:** *And then we have the preheater. Newer preheaters made 1964 and thereafter look like this. (The 'preheater' was called the Rapid Preheater by manufacturers, hence the term 'Rapid' you may see embossed on the font. Lanterns with just an alcohol preheater cup are not 'Rapid.')* ■

■ **ABOVE:** *Preheaters made 1954-1963 look like this.* ■

■ ABOVE: *1941-1953.* ■

■ ABOVE: *1939-1940.* ■

■ **ABOVE:** *1937-1938 Please note that these dates represent info obtained on-line; I cannot testify as to their accuracy. My primary interest is in functionality and light to see with, not dates and model numbers.* ■

What Is a Petromax?

Another question that keeps coming up on Internet forums is, "What's a Petromax? What is it *really*?"

In answer, please know that the Petromax brand name, the trademark, came first and the lantern followed. Today, after all, we are blessed with Coleman ice chests, Coleman collapsible marshmallow sticks, and all manner of other Coleman goodies. Petromax was no different.

Petromax was registered as a trademark in 1910 by Erich and Graetz, a German company. The trademark was used on alcohol lamps, electric lamps, kerosene lamps, wicks, chimneys, portable ovens, and many other items.

After World War II the Petromax trademark was allowed to lapse. It was subsequently reregistered by other companies. Today (2015), in the United States, BriteLyt owns it. Other countries, other owners. The lawyers prosper.

How about the lantern itself?

The first Petromax lantern patent was awarded to Max Graetz in 1912. But there were many patented improvements. By 1928, what we think of today as a 'Petromax' was pretty much in final form and the patents were owned by four different companies: Hugo Schneider AG, Continental-Light AG, J. Hirschhorn AG, and Erich and Graetz AG. (The AG suffix stands for AktienGesellschaft and translates as 'corporation' in English.)

Each of these four companies made their own version of the lantern. Respectively, the lantern brands these companies sold were HASAG, Continental, Aida, and Petromax.

● **HASAG.** stands for 'Hugo Schneider Aktiengesellchaft.' Hugo Schneider was closed down after WWII due to war crimes (use of slave labor). New parts for HASAG lanterns do not exist (or so I am given to understand). Hence, if you want to buy a Petromax-type lantern for lighting (and not for display as a collector's item), HASAG is a poor choice.

● **Continental.** Continental was effectively closed as a company during WWII and only operated after the war in a minor fashion until the owner died in the 1960's.

● **Aida.** The Aida design is actually the mother of the Petromax. Jacob Hirschhorn made the first Petromax-style lantern, the Aida 214, about 1923/24 although the Model

214 did have different parts than a modern, post-WWII Petromax (the check valve, for example).

■ **ABOVE:** *Aida lanterns were embossed with the Hirschhorn logo: a leaping stag with a horn wrapped around its chest. 'Hirsch' in German means stag; 'horn' means horn. Erich and Graetz bought out Hirschhorn in 1928 and thus owned the Hirschhorn trademark from that time forward.* ■

After World War II, Model 1500 Aida lanterns were manufactured alongside Petromax lanterns in the same factory.

Today, 75% of the Aida 1500's on eBay have the 1964-style preheater. All the rest have the 1954 style. This is where the dating, discussed above, is useful. It's a fair bet that all the Aida's you'll find on eBay were made after WWII. In round numbers, that means Petromax parts will fit Aida lanterns. I can testify that the tip (part #50) and pricker (part #68) from a Butterfly (cheap Petromax clone) will fit an Aida with the 1964-style preheater.

As a trademark or brand name, 'Aida' was never farmed out to China. All lanterns branded 'Aida' were made in Europe.

• **Petromax.** Before World War II, Petromax lanterns were made in Germany by Erich and Graetz. After the war, Erich disappeared and Petromax lanterns were made by Graetz AktienGesellschaft and/or Graetz VertriebsGesellschaft.

In the 1970's, Petromax production was licensed to Casa Hipolito SARL in Torres Vedras, Portugal. (SARL stands for *Sociedade Anónima de Responsabilidade Limitada* which translates as 'Limited Liability Company.')

Casa Hipolito made [1] Petromax brand lanterns, [2] Petromax clones sold under the Hipolito brand name, and [3] Petromax clones sold under the Geniol brand name.

It is generally agreed that the lanterns branded 'Hipolito' were fully equal in quality to earlier Petromax lanterns made in Germany. In the 1990's, Casa Hipolito went bankrupt and Petromax production was moved to China.

Like Aida, the Hipolito brand name was never farmed out to China. All Hipolito lanterns were made in Portugal.

■ **ABOVE:** *The Hipolito logo was a sea horse. It was sometimes embossed on the font, sometimes on the ventilator. Excuse me. Make that part #123 'hood with cap.'* ■

Geniol, mentioned above, is another brand of Petromax-style lantern. It was owned by Heinze GMbH of Wuppertal, Germany. Heinze had the Geniol manufactured by Casa Hipolito in Portugal. But, unlike Hipolito or Aida brand lanterns, the 'Geniol' brand *was* farmed out to China. So a Geniol lantern with a 1964-style preheater might have been made in the Far East. Or in Europe. There's no way to tell.

To summarize Petromax itself, lanterns bearing the Petromax trademark were made in Germany before World War II. They were also made in Germany after World War II until the 1970's when production moved to Portugal. They were made in Portugal from the 1970's through the

1990's. All Petromax brand lanterns have been manufactured in China since the 1990's. The patents have long since expired so the Petromax design is freely copied by everyone.

Everyone? Yes, everyone. Petromax brothers, sisters, cousins, and clones include Butterfly (Cixi, China), Butterfly (Lea Hin, Singapore), BriteLyt (USA), Anchor, Sea Anchor, Tower, Santrax, Egret, Solex (Italy), Aida, Geniol, Hipolito (Portugal), Fama, Primus (Sweden), Optimus (Sweden), HASAG, Buflam-Petroflam (England), Aurora (Argentina), Big Wheel, Light, Red Heart, Silveray, Crown (Iraq), Kohinoor (India), Pochee (India), Prabhat (India), Petro Pintsch (Germany), Petrostar (Germany), Solar (China), Standard (Germany), Double Rabbit (Thailand), Cow, Bee, Eye, Glory (China), Yüksel (Turkey), Wenzel (Sam's Club), and Col-Max (USA). Col-Max? Yes. Just before World War II, Coleman began making a Petromax clone for export, intended to directly compete with Petromax itself.

It's dicey. Here's a salient remark from Neil McRae, *Guild Question #2790*: "This enterprising company [Santromax in Hong Kong] makes product for all comers and will stamp on them anything you like. We know they make Petromax and Geniol product for sale in Germany and the US. The Petromax Brand is owned in Germany by Christof Heinze as is Geniol."

Peet van der walt (South Africa), *Guild Question #3404*, says: "Old Pertomax lamps are very good as well but it is not always possible to tell the difference between the old German/Portuguese made once and the newer once made in China." [sic]

So. What to do? What to do?

Well, if you're a purist and want a for-sure made-in-Europe lantern, then buy:
[1] Hipolito,
[2] Aida Model 1500 (the 1500 was manufactured after WWII so parts are compatible),
[3] Petromax with a 1954-style (or earlier) preheater,
[4] Geniol with a 1954-style (or earlier) preheater, or
[5] a German Federal Armed Forces (Bundeswehr) surplus Petromax (to be discussed in a moment).

This group represents the highest quality Petromax lanterns ever made. The downside is that none of these five are cheap. You'll find no bargains here.

FWIW, here's another strategy. From time to time you will find cheap Petromax knockoffs on eBay. It appears that somebody will occasionally buy a whole boatload of Sea Anchor (brand) or Butterfly (brand) or similar cheapie Petromax clones and set out to make his fortune selling them for $50 each on eBay.

So when that happens, buy two. Two brand-new cheapies with the same trademark. Light each one as soon as you get it. Make sure each one runs properly. If not, return it *immediately* for exchange. The idea is to get two, cheap, running, brand new Petromax lanterns of the same brand. Then use one for light and tuck the other away for spare parts.

The lantern you use for light came with spare parts. The lantern you put in storage came with spare parts. Plus the lantern you put in storage *is* spare parts. The result of this strategy is that you'll have a working lantern in brand new condition (that will burn diesel as well as kerosene) plus lots and lots of spare parts. All at a modest price. You should be set for a while.

BriteLyt

OK. Next up is BriteLyt. Think of it as a portal to the Twilight Zone.

BriteLyt, Inc. is owned by Diana Clifton. Actually, Diana is her middle name. Or Diane, really. It should be Julia Diane Clifton. But she's married to a man named Draper. So her legal name is Ms. Julia Diane Clifton Draper. This info is from 'Clifton-Draper v. Pelam International' in Florida. The case had to do with the Petromax trademark. The court document states that, "Silver-Ray Kaipong, a Chinese corporation, sold to the plaintiffs lanterns, cook stoves, and lantern parts, which BriteLyt resold."
http://law.justia.com/cases/federal/district-courts/florida/flmdce/8:2010cv00822/243648/94/

BriteLyt claims its lanterns are 'fifth-generation' Petromax and, more importantly, that BriteLyt lanterns are safe on gasoline. There was a running battle with *The International Guild of Lamp Researchers* for several years on this topic:

> From Diana (Florida), *Guild Question 2492*: "We do, personally, use [flammable] gasoline, on a regular basis, in our BriteLyt-Petromax lanterns, and we do not

sell anyone, anything that we do not use ourselves. So......From my reply from John, I am assuming that he purchased his lantern from GENIOL....is this correct? If you did, then you have the 4th generation Petromax, and it is NOT for use with anything BUT [combustible] kerosene, and, you should have received a letter from that company, advising you of such."

Frankly, the more I research Petromax, the better I understand that the 'fifth generation' narrative is PDF (Pure Diana Fantasy). Perhaps the most significant comment in the whole Guild debate was this:

> From Gerard (Netherlands), *Guild Question 2492*: "...what makes the fith generation safe for the use of gasoline where other petromax-type of lamps are not? Is there a valve added that shuts off fuel-supply thoroughly enough, as in the Coleman-types? If so, the lamp should be safe, otherwise it is not. Can you tel us what changes you made? And, how can we see the difference between generations..." [sic]

A reasonable request, no? And Diana's answer?

What part of *silence* don't you understand?

Petromax in Germany did at one time make a lantern intended for white gas. It was a Model 825, manufactured in the 1930's.

An ordinary Petromax (and that's what the BriteLyt is) has one-knob control. A foot valve down in the tank and a pricker at the tip work in unison to turn fuel on and off. Given a malfunction, you might be in trouble, at least if burning flammable white gas.

So the 1930's gasoline-fueled Model 825 had a separate fuel shutoff valve in addition to its part #111 control knob. The 825 is pictured at http://tgmarsh.faculty.noctrl.edu/ehrichgraetzlant.html. The Work Horse lantern, made by the CJN Adams Corp. in Wellman, Iowa is very similar to the Petromax 825.

■ **ABOVE:** *The Work Horse is a Petromax clone with a separate fuel shutoff valve, intended for white gas as well as kerosene. Unfortunately, Adams Corp. is no longer in business. I say 'unfortunately' because I own a Work Horse and it is truly a superior lantern.* ■

Back to BriteLyt. Advertising hype notwithstanding, BriteLyt lanterns are not of high quality. My BriteLyt, as I mentioned, will not turn completely off. I returned this lantern when it was brand new to BriteLyt in Florida because of the *incredible* quantity of crud in the fuel tank.

They returned it a month later, smelling of methylene chloride, all better.

But now, as it turns out, with the control knob (part #111) in the OFF position, the lantern continues to burn. It will not shut off.

If you Google for BriteLyt, you'll discover a whole new world of griping. The following link is typical: http://www.candlepowerforums.com/vb/showthread.php?8 1693-Petromax-kerosene-lantern-from-BriteLyt

My best advice is to purchase a BriteLyt only where you can for sure return it and get your money back.

You can check out the debate about BriteLyt gasoline safety and five generations and all manner of other good stuff at http://www.lampguild.org/. Here are the question numbers to search for in the Guild archives: #1491, #1945, #2128, #2436, #2438, #2487, #2492, #2496, #2497, #2790, #3105, #3402, #3396, #3404, #4025, #4457, #4655, #4844, #5199, #5724. These entries span a decade (from 2001 to 2011) and total 30,000 words. So it's a book-length discussion. But be warned. Dante's phrase from 700 hundred years ago in the *Divine Comedy* fits perfectly. He described a sign that stood beside the gateway to Hell: "Abandon all hope, ye who enter here."

Let me summarize. Design issues exist that shout NO to the use of gasoline in any Petromax. And that includes BriteLyt (which is, after all, just another Petromax clone). But can you burn gas in a BriteLyt and get away with it? Of course. And can you pump gas into your car while smoking a cigarette and get away with it? Of course. I've seen people do it for years and I've never seen a fire. Then again, check out 'gas pump smoking' on YouTube.

German Army Surplus

The traditional Petromax, discussed above, has a Preston-loop generator and was designed for kerosene.

In the 1950's and 1960's the German Bundeswehr (Federal Armed Forces) used Petromax lanterns made in Altena, Germany. One army model, the 829 500HK, had a Preston loop and was designed for kerosene. Another model, the 829B 500HK, had a straight generator that resembled a Coleman generator.

In a lantern designated 829B, the 'B' stands for benzin, the German word for gasoline. So the '829' is a kerosene lantern and the '829B' is a gasoline lantern. The difference between the two is the generator style.

These lanterns used an HK (HefnerKerze) rating rather than CP (candlepower). One HK is 0.91 of a candlepower. So a 500HK lantern equals 455CP.

About 1960-61, the German army was forced to follow a civilian rule that forbade 'gasoline-driven' devices in houses and tents (ref. *Guild Question #2492*). It appears, however, that lanterns already in inventory were not scrapped; many if not all were retrofitted and/or re-marked.

About ten years ago eBay was flooded with German army surplus lanterns. Many came with metal cases. And the markings on the cases often contradicted the markings on the lantern. And the markings on the lantern often contradicted the actual generator mounted on the lantern.

So the lantern you just bought on eBay for $300 . . . *what is it?* Well, if it has a Preston loop it is a kerosene lantern. If it has a straight generator, it is set up for gasoline. Can it be set up in a way that contradicts the badge or label? Of course.

Let me repeat. This new lantern you just bought . . . what is it? Look at the generator. Ignore the badge. Ignore what is stenciled on the box.

Imagine this. (Allow me a bit of speculation here. I'm going to indulge in some 'writer's license.') Imagine you just won at auction a lot of 900 (German) army surplus Petromax lanterns. Some have generators mounted on them, some don't. Some are badged 829 and some are badged 829B. What a mess. But you got them really cheap.

Now you can peddle those 750 army-surplus metal lantern boxes you bought last month. Some of those boxes are stenciled petroleum (kerosene) and some are stenciled benzin (gasoline) and some have 'benzin' painted out and 'petroleum' stenciled in its place. *And* you can get rid of those 200 army surplus generators that have been gathering dust in the back room since before the First Gulf War.

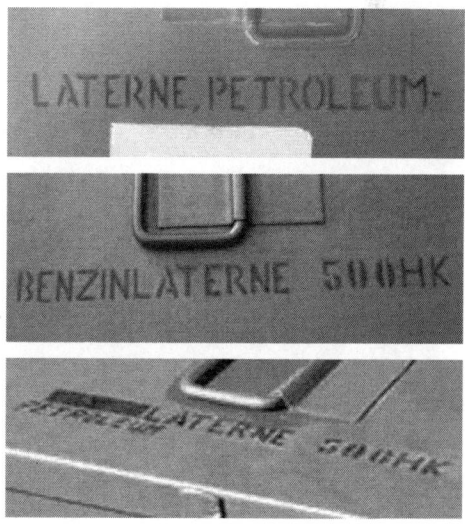

These army surplus lanterns were made in Germany circa 1960. They are higher quality than anything coming out of the China today. But they are mix-and-match as far as parts and labeling are concerned.

Is it safe to burn *kerosene* in a Petromax set up for kerosene (i.e. with a Preston loop)? Answer. Yes, of course.

Is it safe to burn *kerosene* in a Petromax set up for gasoline (i.e. with a straight generator)? Answer. Not really. Most likely the straight-line generator won't get hot enough to vaporize the fuel properly and you'll have constant flare-ups.

■ **ABOVE:** *This lantern, with its Preston loop, is set up for kerosene although the 'B' on its badge indicates benzin (gasoline).* ■

■ **ABOVE:** *This lantern, with its straight generator, is set up for gasoline. Except for the dates, this lantern and the one above are badged identically. According to their labels, both are 829B. "B" stands for benzin. Benzin is the German word for gasoline.* ■

Is it safe to burn *gasoline* in a Petromax set up for kerosene? No. (Despite what BriteLyt may claim.) Why? For the various reasons mentioned in this book plus other design issues detailed by Neil McRae at www.petromax.nl/petromax_tale/petromax_myth.html.

Is it safe to burn *gasoline* in a Petromax set up for gasoline? No. *For all the same reasons.*

BTW. If you have one of these Bundeswehr lanterns with a 'straight' gasoline generator, you can replace that generator with a Preston-loop generator (part #152). Then you'll have the real deal.

And it doesn't have to be a Petromax-brand #152. The #152 can be Wenzel-brand or Geniol-brand or salvaged from a damaged Aida. That's the beauty of the Petromax design. It's the same worldwide irrespective of brand name. And it's been that way since World War II if not longer.

It's machining tolerances and adherence to spec that makes the difference between a high quality Petromax and what I'm calling a cheapie. The difference is not in the design. Or even in the materials. After all, a cheapie Butterfly *weighs* the same as a top-drawer Hipolito. Rather, the quality issue is exemplified by shallow threads produced on worn tooling versus crisp threads from new tooling.

Preheating

We need to discuss some practical aspects of operating a Petromax. First up is preheating.

Preheating a Petromax with alcohol is basically the same as preheating a Coleman. One difference is that a Petromax lantern must be fully assembled (with the glass globe in place) before alcohol preheating can occur. The glass globe goes on first, *then* the U-shaped mixing tube. You can't light a Petromax first and install the glass later.

Preheating with an alcohol cup takes four minutes; with a Rapid Preheater, 90 seconds. Admittedly, the Rapid Preheater is a bit rough on the mantles but it does make a manly roaring sound. Sometimes I think that the roar is its biggest market appeal. "Me Tarzan. Listen to my *roar!*"

There are several 'how to light a Petromax using the Rapid Preheater' videos on YouTube:

https://www.youtube.com/watch?v=P7S1A6eeK7Q
https://www.youtube.com/watch?v=WcgPVRIEFPo
https://www.youtube.com/watch?v=pMJDaokLHeI
https://www.youtube.com/watch?v=nI27kp-1ALk

To use a preheater, the steps are these:

(1) Put in fuel, tighten the fuel cap (i.e. manometer, part #149), and pump in 1.5 bars of pressure.

(2) Light a kitchen match or light a butane torch or light a cigarette lighter.

(3) Open the 'tilt lever,' part #223, by pushing down on it. Immediately apply your flame to the spray of fuel. Be cool. It really does make a roar. Leave the 'tilt lever' open.

■ **ABOVE (L to R):** *Tilt lever closed. Tilt lever open.* ■

(4) Run the (roaring) preheater for 90 seconds. Pump the lantern during that time, while the preheater is running, and keep the pressure at 1.5 bars.

(5) After 90 seconds, turn the control knob (part #111) so that the arrow points down (sending fuel to the mantle).

(6) Raise the 'tilt lever' to turn off the preheater.

(7) CONTRARY TO WHAT IS DEMONSTRATED ON YOUTUBE, DO THIS OUTSIDE, NOT AT THE KITCHEN SINK!

Pumping in Pressure

The hand pumps that come factory-installed on Petromax lanterns leave a lot to be desired. In principle they are the same as Coleman pumps but, in practice, Petromax pumps are nearly useless. (BTW, Coleman 'pump cups' are larger in diameter than Petromax and will not fit a Petromax. The Petromax pump cup is part #46.)

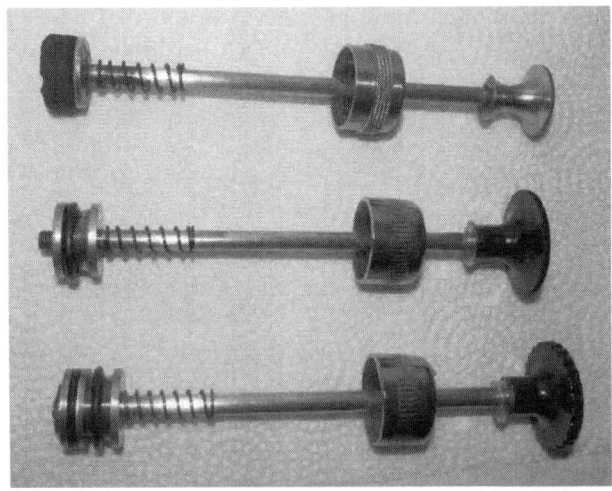

■ **ABOVE:** *I did a comparison test of three Petromax pump designs. The pump at the top is from an old Hipolito. The leather had obviously not been used in years. I picked off the dried crud and dipped it in a jar of neatsfoot oil before starting the test. It should have been soaked overnight but all it got was a quick dip. The pump in the middle has one rubber O-ring and is from a brand new Butterfly lantern. The pump at the bottom has two rubber O-rings and is a brand new BriteLyt pump.* ■

I used the same lantern (a new Butterfly) for all three tests. I chose that particular lantern because its foot valve worked very smoothly; it readily accepted pressure. The foot valve on many Petromax lanterns is fitful and jerky; inspiring user-confidence is not a strong suit.

I also chose a manometer (combo fuel cap and pressure gauge) that worked smoothly and consistently. I used the same manometer (part #149) for all three tests. After each test I set the lantern aside for a couple of hours. In all cases the lantern held pressure for the duration; it did not ebb away. That confirmed the lantern was accepting (and holding) pressure properly back when I was pumping.

The results surprised me. The old Hipolito pump with the leather pump cup brought the (empty) lantern to 1.5 bars of pressure in 150 strokes. The Butterfly pump with one O-ring took 400 strokes. The BriteLyt pump with two O-rings required 550 strokes. I replaced the rear-most BriteLyt O-ring with one that was slightly larger. It then took 800 strokes.

No? Then you do it. I dare you. *Double-dare.*

FYI, to make sure I didn't lose count (easy enough to do when the count climbs into the hundreds), every time I pumped in a hundred strokes I tore a paper match out of a matchbook and dropped it in a cup on the workbench. And rested my thumb for a bit.

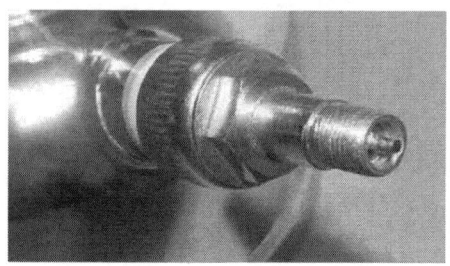

■ **ABOVE:** *This adaptor is sold by BriteLyt. It's shown here mounted on a BriteLyt lantern (although it fits any brand of Petromax). It replaces the original, factory-installed pump. The Britelyt threads were not the best so I used Teflon tape to get a good seal. With this adaptor in place (which is actually a Schrader valve such as you have on a bicycle tube) you can use a tire pump to pressurize your Petromax.* ■

■ **ABOVE:** *This is an even better arrangement. It's a Schrader valve built into a manometer. It comes factory-installed on Work Horse and Menno-Miser (brand) lanterns but I have on occasion seen it sold separately on eBay. It sidesteps any finicky foot valve problems and therefore allows you to pump in air very smoothly.* ■

■ **ABOVE:** *This is a conventional manometer (no Schrader valve). The thumb screw is a needle valve that releases pressure.* ■

The manometer is one reason flammable Coleman fuel is not safe in a Petromax; there's a certain amount of vaporized fuel in the air being released and it's very close to a glowing mantle. If you somehow get caught in that situation (for example, I was running a BriteLyt set up for alcohol, another flammable fuel, and the lantern refused to shut off), you can use your hand as a shield between the thumbscrew and the glass globe as well as blowing on the exiting air to decrease the fuel concentration in the air. Or you could fashion a bigger shield from cardboard or aluminum foil instead of using your hand. Or use a folded newspaper as a fan.

Air Gap Adjustment

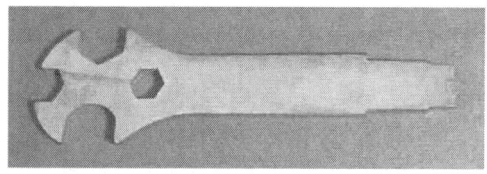

■ **ABOVE:** *This is the free wrench that comes with a new Petromax.* ■

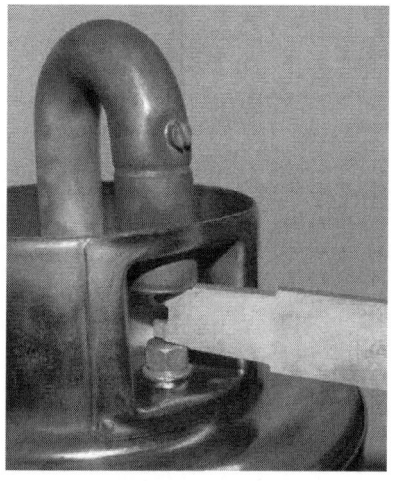

For a 500CP Petromax, the air gap should be set at 14.2 mm. The smaller steps on the wrench/gauge are for smaller lanterns (300CP, 200CP, etc.). It's a good idea to measure your wrench/gauge with a ruler before adjusting the lantern to be sure you're on the correct step ($^9/_{16}$" is 14.28 mm).

Pricker Adjustment

Sometimes a new lantern comes from the store adjusted such that the pricker protrudes out of the tip too far. *Much* too far. According to folks in the know, the pricker, when fully extended, should only stick out of the tip 0.5 to 1.0 mm, just enough to snag your thumbnail.

Here's how the adjustment is made.

> **Note.** I've used proper Petromax part numbers to avoid ambiguity but have not included a diagram showing those part numbers because such a chart would be too small to be legible on Kindle. The good news is that Petromax diagrams are widely available. All new lanterns come with a part-number diagram and Google will find hundreds for you. It might be a good idea, in fact, to locate one now and print it out before you need it i.e. before TSHTF.

To adjust the pricker, we must do some disassembling. First, we remove the hood or ventilator (part #123) and the U-tube (assembly #125) and the glass globe (part #74) and the heat shield (part #126). You likely don't need pictures to get that far.

104

■ **ABOVE:** *Next, we remove the screw (part #21), indicated by the arrow in the above photo, and lift off the entire support frame (part #121) including the center ring (part #122) and alcohol cup (part #35).* ■

■ **ABOVE:** *At this point the lantern is starting to look stripped down (as shown in the above photo) but nothing, really, has been removed that isn't quite easy to put back.* ■

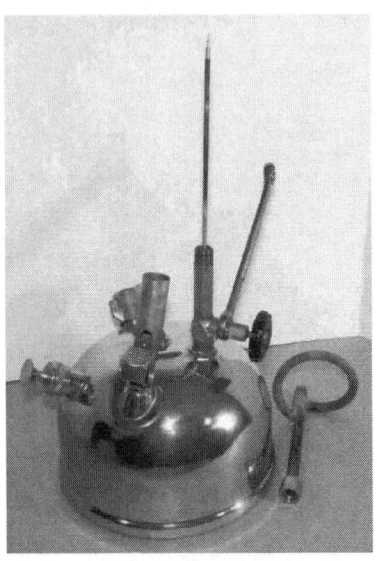

■ **ABOVE:** *We remove the Preston loop, part #152, shown here lying on its side. After that, the eccentric (assembly #114) must be removed from the lower part of the carburetor (part #153). Until we remove the eccentric, the stud on the eccentric prevents the removal of the guide rod/valve rod (assembly #104). The photo above shows a wrench in position for eccentric removal.* ■

■ **ABOVE:** *To be clear, the wrench is placed on the fitting shown above (part #107).* ■

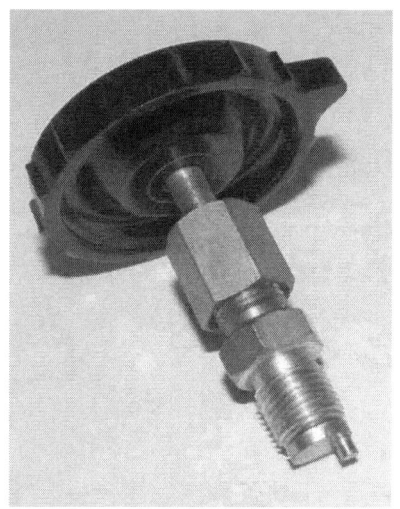

■ **ABOVE:** *Here we see assembly #114 after being removed from the lantern. The part that makes this assembly an 'eccentric' is the off-center stud shown in the lower right-hand corner of the photo. That stud fits in a slot in part #103 (the 'receiver') which is one section of the 'whole generator rod' (assembly #104).* ■

■ **ABOVE:** *Once the eccentric assembly #114 is removed, we can simply lift the guide rod (part #101) and the valve rod (part #191) out of the lantern. They are joined together by the receiver (part #103) making them one long piece (assembly #104). On the left end (if it's not too small to see), I did not remove the pricker (part #68) from the guide rod. No need.* ■

■ **ABOVE:** *Here we see the slotted receiver (part #103). On the left side is the valve rod (part #191) that goes down inside the font. On the right side is the guide rod (part #101) that has the pricker attached. The threaded portion of the guide rod is where the length adjustment occurs. Screwing or unscrewing the guide rod from the receiver determines how far out of the tip the pricker protrudes. On the threaded portion you can see a jam nut or locknut (part #102). The jam nut prevents the length adjustment from changing once it has been made.* ■

■ **ABOVE:** *We back off the jam nut and screw the guide rod into the receiver a few turns. This is a trial-and-error process. After making what we think is the appropriate adjustment, we reassemble the lantern (finger tight) and check our results. If need be, we disassemble the lantern and repeat the procedure. Sooner or later we're bound to get it right, eh?* ■

■ **ABOVE:** *Here's the one tricky part of the whole process. It's the remounting of the eccentric (assembly #114) onto the lower part of the carburetor (part #153).* ■

We must line up the eccentric stud with the receiver slot.

To start, we slide assembly #104 (that is, #101 guide rod plus #103 receiver plus #191 valve rod) into the carburetor (part #153). The end with the pricker is 'up.'

We rotate assembly #104 so that the slot in the receiver faces forward; we can look in the hole and see it (as in the photo above).

The lower end of the valve rod, down inside the font, rests on a spring-loaded foot valve. If we push down on the guide rod, we can compress the spring and push the receiver slot lower in the hole.

Next we screw in assembly #114 (the eccentric). We stop as soon as we feel the stud make contact with the receiver. We push down on the guide rod, thereby lowering the receiver slot to make it more accessible, and jiggle (for lack of a better word) the guide rod and the eccentric until the stud enters the slot. We can feel it when it happens; it's more complicated to describe than it is to do.

At this point we can resume screwing in the eccentric assembly (#114). The pricker moves up and down as we tighten but that's okay; with the stud in the slot, that's what it's supposed to do.

Finally we remount the Preston loop (and the tip) and check our results. If the lantern is good-to-go then we need to back up a few steps and tighten everything. If not good-to-go, then we disassemble everything for another iteration.

Now tell me the truth. Isn't this fun?

Wire Mesh Globe

The purpose of a globe (part #74) is to protect the mantle from flying insects attracted to the light. A lantern will run without a globe but the run time may be short. Buzz, buzz.

It is quite feasible to use a wire mesh globe instead of glass. For the 500CP Petromax size, mesh globes are sold on eBay for about $30 including postage. They are made of stainless steel. They do cut light transmission to some degree.

I have not seen a wire mesh globe sized for a Coleman but certainly one could be fashioned.

Just another idea that may prove useful in a SHTF scenario.

ALADDIN

Introduction

The Aladdin lamp is a love/hate device. Enough good ones were produced over the past hundred years to spawn a world-wide collectors' club, The Aladdin Knights of the Mystic Light. Enough bad ones were produced to keep eBay in business for the next hundred years.

Aladdins burn kerosene. They are easy to light, comparable to simple flat-wick lamps. They don't flicker. They can provide up to 60 watts-worth of steady, white light. Not being pressurized, they don't hiss. As mantle lamps, they burns 99% of all volatiles and therefore have minimal smell. The low-smell, no-hiss, and no-flicker factors make Aladdins hard to beat.

■ **ABOVE:** *Back in the day, Aladdins were upscale lamps with fancy glass globes. The Model 23 Genie (above) has a paper shade and a pressed glass font for economy. The Model 23 has been in production since 1969 but has a spotty quality record. Today (2015) it's on the verge being replaced with the MAXbrite 500. That's a major development.* ■

A theme developed in the course of this writing this Aladdin section. Well, not a theme exactly. Something more like a puzzle. I think you'll see it as we go along.

The conundrum is this. What's the ultimate regulator of Aladdin light output? What clinches the deal? Is it the lamp? Or is it the mantle? And the answer is 'yes.'

First, I have a Model B Aladdin lamp that produces 75 watts-worth of light on an old-time British-made (thorium) mantle but only 40 watts-worth on a newer Brazil-made (thorium) mantle. So given the same lamp, two different mantles produce two different levels of illumination. It's clearly the *mantle* that determines light output.

But Galen Lehman (whom we'll meet in a moment) says he has a Phillipine-made yttrium mantle that gives 60 candlepower on a Model B Aladdin lamp but only 15 candlepower on a Model 23 'star' lamp. So given the same mantle, two different lamps produce two different levels of illumination. It's clearly the *lamp* that determines light output. This was not an easy chapter to write.

History

In 1908, Victor Samuel Johnson incorporated the Mantle Lamp Company of America. In 1949 the name was changed to Aladdin Industries. A lamp division still existed but Aladdin Industries branched out far beyond kerosene lamps. At one point, Hopalong Cassidy lunch boxes were a big seller. You DO remember Hopalong Cassidy, yes?

Aladdin Models

Model 1: 1909-1910
Model 2: 1910
Model 3: 1911-12
Model 4: 1912-13
Model 5: 1913-14
Model 6: 1914-17
Model 7: 1917-19
Model 8: 1919-20
Model 9: 1920-22
Model 10: 1921-22
Model 11: 1922-28
Model 12: 1928-35
Model A: 1932
Model B: 1933-55 (22 years)
Model C: 1955-63
Model 21: 1953-63 (made in England)
Model 21C: 1963-69 (made in England)
Model 23: 1969-2015 (made in England until 1977; in Hong Kong thereafter)
MAXbrite 500: 2015-

Source: *Aladdin, The Magic Name in Lamps*, J.W. Courter

■ **ABOVE:** *Starting in 1913 with the Model 5, an Aladdin's model number appears on its wick-wheel.* ■

"Through much of the 1970s, '80s and going into the '90s [this equates to the Model 23 if you review the above list] Aladdin had been outsourcing to low cost manufacturers who just were not making parts that fit or worked well. Expensive lamps were being offered for sale that often did not fit or work quite right. It seemed that Aladdin Industries just did not want to discontinue its root business nor did it want to spend the money and effort to revitalize it. The Aladdin lamp division seemed to be sliding slowly towards oblivion as the lamps slowly faded from public memory. By 1998, Aladdin's lamp division profits were around 1% of the Aladdin Industries annual income." *TeriAnns Guide to Aladdin and other brands of kerosene Mantle Lamps* http://www.aladdinlamps.info/history.htm

In 1999, Aladdin Industries sold its lamp division to a group of Aladdin collectors. The collectors formed the Aladdin Mantle Lamp Company.

Later, the Aladdin Mantle Lamp Company changed its name to Aladdin Lighting Technologies.

Crownplace Brands bought Aladdin Lighting Technologies and took over production in February 2015.

"Most of the [lamp] inventory we [Crownplace] currently carry was inherited from the old Aladdin company. We did a quality control inspection upon receipt and rejected thousands of dollars worth of product. That means that the lamps we produce will be higher quality right out of the gate.

"Aladdin Lighting Technologies [the previous owner] began work on a new burner about three years ago, which we are completing. The new burner, called

MAXbrite, will be available . . . sometime this year." –
Galen Lehman, President, Crownplace Brands, August
2015.

New owner? That's a game-changer. The first new model
in 46 years? An even bigger game-changer.

Model 23

When I first became interested in emergency lighting
(resulting from the 2003 blackout of the Northeast U.S.),
the Aladdin became my lamp of choice. Upon retiring in
2005 I bought a Model 23, a dozen Brazilian-made mantles
(thorium), a dozen Malta-made mantles (yttrium), a dozen
wicks, and six extra chimneys.

The specific lamp I purchased turned out to be a good one
but I later discovered it was luck of the draw. The
manufacture of Model 23's had been transferred to Hong
Kong in 1977 and collectors were not at all happy with
Hong-Kong quality.

Contributors to *The International Guild of Lamp
Researchers* advised readers to replace their Hong-Kong
burners with English-made burners. *Guild Questions #3193
and #4125*. There's a practical difficulty, however, in
following that advice. Although English-made burners are
available on www.ebay.co.uk/, it seems that most U.K.
sellers don't ship internationally.

A couple of years after buying my Model 23 it began to
appear that Aladdin lamps might go the way of eight-track
tape players. I advised friends that, if they wanted to go the
Aladdin route, they should "get a good model and lay in a
supply of spare parts."

A good model, you say? And which one is that? It's a tough question because Aladdin's quality record is a hit-and-miss affair.

■ **ABOVE:** *The Model 23 'star.'* ■

J.W. Courter, author of Aladdin, *The Magic Name in Lamps*, admitted that some Model 23's made in Hong Kong "do not burn very well." But he insisted that today's 'star' burner (identified by the five-point star embossed on the lamp's collar) "can perform as well as the best." He made that remark in 2005. *Guild Question #3193.*

It was a self-serving assertion because six years earlier, "On 5 April 1999 a group of Aladdin enthusiasts headed by J.W. Courter and Tom Teeter purchased the Aladdin mantle lamp division from Aladdin Industries [and started the Aladdin Mantle Lamp Company]." **TeriAnns Guide to Aladdin and other brands of kerosene Mantle Lamps** www.aladdinlamps.info/history.htm

The Model 23 'star' thus produced current revenue for Courter's company. That being the case, what would you expect Courter to say? "I recommend that you don't buy anything we make or sell. It's not very good. I recommend you buy stuff that Aladdin produced thirty years ago.

Second-hand stuff. It's much better than what we're selling today."

Of late, I came in contact with Galen Lehman, an Aladdin collector as well as President of Crownplace Brands (who recently acquired Aladdin Lighting Technologies). Galen wrote me: "The best thing I can say about any #23 burner, in summary, is that the quality was inconsistent. One of the Aladdin collectors told me that he has two #23 burners. Using the same '40 cp' Philippine mantle on both burners, he gets 23 cp from one and 60 cp from the other!"

Further, Galen recommended the Model B burner: "Might I suggest a #B burner . . . I think the Model B will outperform all the others. Certainly, the #B is held out as 'the best' by many collectors. Personally, getting to 'Model B performance' is my ultimate goal [for our new generation of Aladdin lamps]."

For me, that finally answered the question, "Which one is a good one?" And Model B's are not truly rare. Some four million were produced between 1933 and 1955. That's 3500 a week for 22 years. There's always a few on eBay.

But, you ask, if the Model B is so good, then why do we need to talk about the Model 23 at all? Because there's so doggone many of them. Because they've been in production for 46 years. Because, whether it's Lehman's catalog, the hardware store, or eBay, the Model 23 is what you'll find. No matter where you go, you'll likely come home with a Model 23.

I did.

My Model 23 outputs 60 watts-worth of light. Oops! Once again I said *watts* whereas Galen talks *candlepower*. Let's clarify that before going further.

Candlepower & Watts

Lumens are a measure of the total amount of light emitted by a source in all directions.

Candlepower is a measure of illumination emitted in one direction. One candlepower in all directions produces 12.57 lumens (for the mathematically inclined, 12.57 is equivalent to '4 pi' and 'pi' is the ratio of a circle's circumference to its diameter).

A common incandescent light bulb throws off light in all directions. One *watt* of electrical input produces 15 lumens of light output.

A **100-watt** light bulb thus produces 1500 lumens (100 x 15 = 1500) or **119 candlepower** (1500 ÷ 12.57 = 119). We've gone from *watts* to *lumens* to *candlepower*.

Similarly, a **40-candlepower** mantle produces 502.8 lumens (40 x 12.57 = 502.8) or **33.5 watts** (502.8 ÷ 15 = 33.5). We've gone in reverse order from *candlepower* to *lumens* to *watts*.

As a practical matter, I compare lamps and lanterns using *watts* as the measure of illumination. Including 3-way bulbs, I have a fair range of light bulb wattages for visual comparison (4, 5, 7, 7½, 15, 25, 30, 40, 50, 60, 70, 75, 100, 135, 150, 200, 240, 250, and 300).

It's a simple, real-world approach. When in doubt, I call in the neighbor's kid for a second opinion.

■ **ABOVE:** *The neighbor's kid.* ■

How the Aladdin Works

■ **ABOVE:** *The Aladdin is not pressurized. It uses a tubular wick, an inch in diameter, with its flame positioned under a mantle. A wick can be expected to last 1000 hours.* ■

■ **ABOVE:** *It's the mantle that provides light, not the flame. The wire frame supporting the cloth mantle is called a 'harp.' Aladdin mantles are preformed and rigid. They must be 'fired' before their first use but they do not shrink in the firing as do Coleman sock-style mantles.* ■

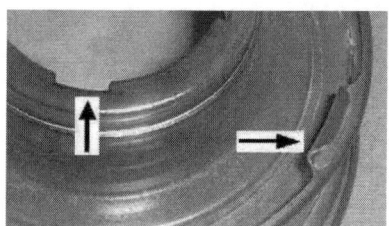

■ **ABOVE:** *The notches in the gallery hold a 'Lox-On' mantle; the tabs (outer edge) hold a 'Lox-On' chimney.* ■

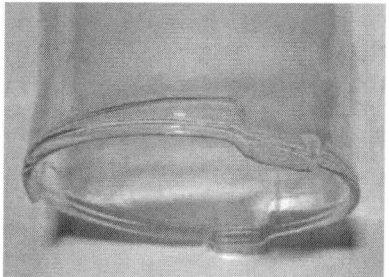

■ **ABOVE:** *A Lox-On chimney. The base of the chimney has (glass) cast-in feet plus (glass) 'wedges' between the feet. The*

feet slide under the metal tabs in the gallery. After that, turning the chimney clockwise engages the wedges and tightens the chimney in place. ■

■ **ABOVE:** *Turn the gallery upside down and you can see four tiny tabs that hold the mantle in place.* ■

■ **ABOVE:** *Here we see the unitized gallery, mantle, and chimney. In the lighting process this subassembly is handled as one piece.* ■

■ **ABOVE:** *One subassembly is the font-burner-wick. The other subassembly is the gallery-mantle-chimney.* **Don't lay it down as shown here! Take care of that mantle!** ■

■ **ABOVE:** *Light the wick, just as you would any wick-type lamp, then mount the gallery sub-assembly. The Lox-On design is a clever piece of engineering. Unfortunately, interchangeability of parts is not a strong suit between Aladdin models.* ■

■ **ABOVE:** *Hooked and leveled, ready to rock. Run it on low for 20 minutes before cranking it up.* ■

Tom Teeter recommends ten minutes of warmup. www.youtube.com/watch?v=5chy_elW85E

In an email to me, Galen Lehman said, "In our testing, we've found that the burner usually takes 20 minutes to reach equilibrium temperature."

Personally, the longer I play around with Aladdin lamps, the more I favor the extended 20-minute warmup. When, after 20 minutes, you finally do bring the lamp up to cruising altitude, I think the performance is better plus you avoid flare-ups that can result from insufficient preheating.

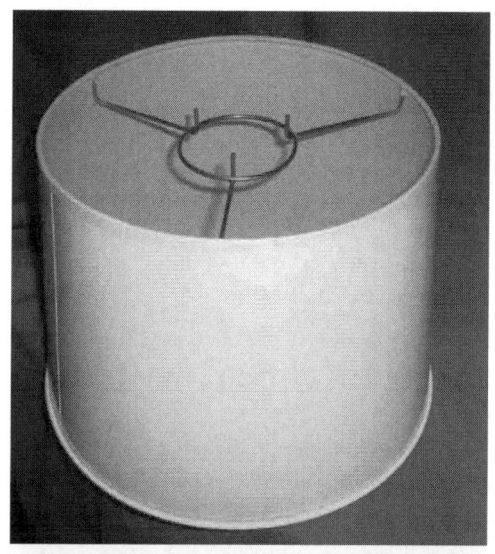

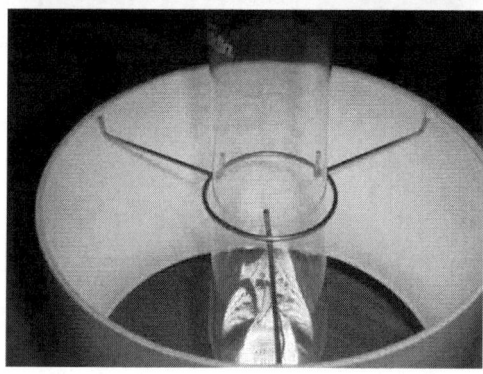

■ **ABOVE:** *Most Aladdins use a glass shade. This economy paper shade ($17) is an exception. It hangs directly on the chimney and is 100% supported by the chimney. It will work on any model.* ■

Aladdin Lamp Fuel

■ **ABOVE:** *It appears that Aladdin Lamp FUEL has replaced Aladdin Lamp OIL (different label). Aladdin recommends using only Aladdin Lamp Fuel or K1 kerosene in an Aladdin lamp. K1 kerosene is for non-vented appliances (lanterns) and contains 400 ppm (parts per million) sulfur. K2 kerosene is for vented appliances (furnaces with a chimney) and contains 3000 ppm sulfur. Sulfur is where the smell comes from.* ■

Speaking of The Non-Electric Lighting Series, here's an excerpt from *Book 3: Lamp Fuels.*

"There is never total agreement on these things. Aladdin lamps in particular provoke a lot of fuel-related discussion.

"The Aladdin Knights, a group of dedicated Aladdin collectors, say, 'Other fuels which have been tried successfully are Lamplight Farms *Ultra-Pure* lamp oil . . .' http://www.aladdinknights.org/faq.php

"The Aladdin Mantle Lamp Company recommends against using *Ultra-Pure* fuel in Aladdins. (Then again, the Aladdin Mantle Lamp Company sells its own competing brand of lamp fuel.) www.aladdinlamps.com/ViewPage.asp?PadeID=2

" 'I used *Ultra-Pure* . . . exclusively in all my kero lamps for years [including Aladdin] . . . [Aladdin Mantle Lamp Company's] lack of recommendation is pure BS' (Fil Graff, Aladdin Knight, The International Guild of Lamp Researchers, question 2442)

"Lamplight Farms, the makers of *Ultra-Pure*, says, 'Use Lamplight® Regular lamp oil for your Aladdin lamp. You cannot use Ultra-Pure® as it will cause premature failure of the mantle material.' www.lamplight.com/Consumer/KnowledgeBase.aspx?KnowledgeID=2233

"With all the brouhaha I decided a test was in order. So I ran my trusty Aladdin [Model 23] for one full evening on *Ultra-Pure* ($32/gallon); then for an evening on *Klean-Strip Klean-Heat* ($11/gallon); then on *Aladdin* brand lamp fuel ($19/gallon); then on *odorless mineral spirits* ($12-18/gallon); and finally on *K-1 kerosene* (the stuff with the red dye in it) from the local gas station ($4/gallon).

"The procedure was to fill and light the lamp outside on the breezeway, let it warm up for 20 minutes on the breezeway, then take it inside and place it in the middle of the dining room table. Several hours later the still-burning lamp was taken back to the breezeway where it was extinguished and allowed to cool. Results? Truth time . . . you could not smell any of them in the house . . . even the cheap stuff with the red dye . . .

"You take it from there."

Someone mentioned to me that *Ultra-Pure* is thicker, more viscous, than Aladdin fuel or kerosene and, although *Ultra-Pure* works satisfactorily in the beginning of a burn, at the end (where the wick must lift it further) it will not perform well. Supporting that notion, the MSDS sheet for *Ultra-Pure* does show a higher viscosity than kerosene (2.5-2.7 cSt for *Ultra-Pure* versus 1.0-2.4 cSt for kerosene).

And what is cSt? Centistokes. That clears everything up, eh?

Actually, my own experience is that the font gets warmer and the fuel gets thinner as the burn continues. The result is that *Ultra-Pure* works fine from beginning to end.

The Lamplight Farms' caution about mantle failure is probably based on the fact that the flash point of *Ultra-Pure* is 250° F whereas Aladdin fuel is only 141° F. Likely the conjecture is made that a higher flash point equates to a higher flame temperature which, in turn, is rough on the mantle. But is that indeed the line of reasoning? And was it ever tested? Or is it just armchair science?

To check it out, I did a comparison of two identical flat-wick lamps, one burning Aladdin fuel, the other, *Ultra-Pure*. (This is the same kind of comparison I made between kerosene and mineral spirits in *Book 3: Lamp Fuels*.)

It's the glowing carbon particles in a lamp's flame that produce light, that allow you to see the flame. The whiter the light, the hotter the flame. The more orange the light, the cooler the flame.

I asked my wife to judge which flame was whiter. Not bigger or brighter but *whiter*. Unknown to her was which lamp burned which fuel. She chose the Aladdin fuel as producing the whiter flame. I chose the *Ultra-Pure*. What we proved was that they are surprisingly close.

While on the topic of lamp fuel, how about diesel? How would diesel fuel perform in an Aladdin lamp? I tried it out in my Model 35 with a new Philippine-made mantle (to be discussed in a moment). Initially I ran it at 60 watts-worth of light output. After two hours at that level it developed a carbon spot on the mantle. I turned it back to a 40-watt level and burned off the black spot, after which it coasted along just fine for several hours at 40 watts.

SAFETY. Note that both diesel and *Ultra-Pure* are combustible liquids with flash points above 100° F. (How they perform as lamp fuels is not the point. As combustible liquids they are not explosion hazards, either one of them. THAT'S the point.) Please don't try *flammable* liquids (gasoline or Coleman fuel) in an Aladdin or any other wick-type lamp. Flammable liquids have flash points below 100° F.

Do you really and truly understand the difference between *flammable* and *combustible*? Earlier I said: "Now riddle me this. How will setting the kitchen curtains on fire in the middle of a blackout make life easier?" Well, okay, how about burning the house down? For me, the most important part of 'being prepared' is knowing what you're doing. And, I regret to inform you, survival knowledge is not the same as winning 'trivia night' at the local bar-and-grill.

Operating Tip

■ **ABOVE:** *Flame spreader. Back in the beginning, what we now call a 'flame spreader' Aladdin called a 'generator.' They changed the name to flame spreader in the early 1920's but you'll still occasionally see the term 'generator' in Aladdin literature today.* ■

Before saying a burner is doesn't work:

● If only the top of the mantle is glowing, then the flame spreader is too low and needs to be raised.

● If only the bottom is glowing, the flame spreader needs to be lowered.

● If only one side of the mantle glows, the wire harp needs to be bent so as to center the mantle over the flame.

High-Altitude Chimney

They say the air is 'thin' at higher altitudes. It would be more 'scientifical' to say the concentration of oxygen is lower. And the amount of oxygen impacts lamp combustion and light output.

To compensate for the thin air, Aladdin sells a high-altitude chimney. It's $15^1/_2$" tall versus the regular height of $12^1/_2$". It's recommended for altitudes from 4,000 to 8,000 feet above sea level. I've also seen homemade chimney extensions fashioned out of aluminum foil.

A taller chimney increases the draft, and thus the air supply, and thus the oxygen supply, to the flame. But increased draft has a chilling effect on flame temperature. So there's a practical limit as to how high an extension is useful.

Galen Lehman advises that (for the majority of us who live closer to sea level) a high-altitude chimney will increase an Aladdin's light output by 15-20%. Lehman's on-line catalog store plans to rename its 'high-altitude' chimney as a 'high output' chimney.

Having lived near sea level all my life, I truthfully never thought about a high-altitude chimney. And, not wanting to shell out $30 for a high-altitude chimney or even $20 for a 'light-booster' extension, I ventured down to the shop to see what I could improvise.

A lamp chimney is essentially a piece of glass tubing. It's 'fire polished' on the end so that nobody gets cut. But that means the glass was briefly molten and that a bump formed when it cooled. The bump prevents any end-to-end butt joint from forming a perfect seal.

I decided to use a small tin can (I think pineapple juice came in it) for the extender. I then discovered that different chimneys had different diameters. On one, the can's diameter and the chimney's diameter were identical. That matchup created a butt joint.

Another chimney was smaller in diameter and slid inside the can. So I cut one end such that a lip remained around the edge (upon which the can could rest atop the chimney). The pictures below will hopefully clarify.

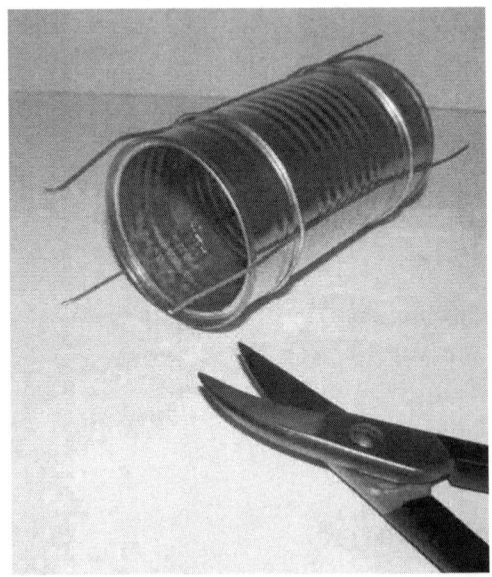

■ **ABOVE:** *I used small, curved tin snips (you can buy these at a craft store) and cut out one end of the can leaving a lip or flange around the edge. That end is facing you, above, and will be used with the smaller-diameter chimney. The far end is simply opened with a can opener and will form a butt joint with the larger-diameter chimney. There are three wires serving as legs to hold the extender in place no matter which end of the can is put in service. The wire legs are themselves held in place with two tie-wires that go around the can. The tie-wire ends are twisted together with pliers.* ■

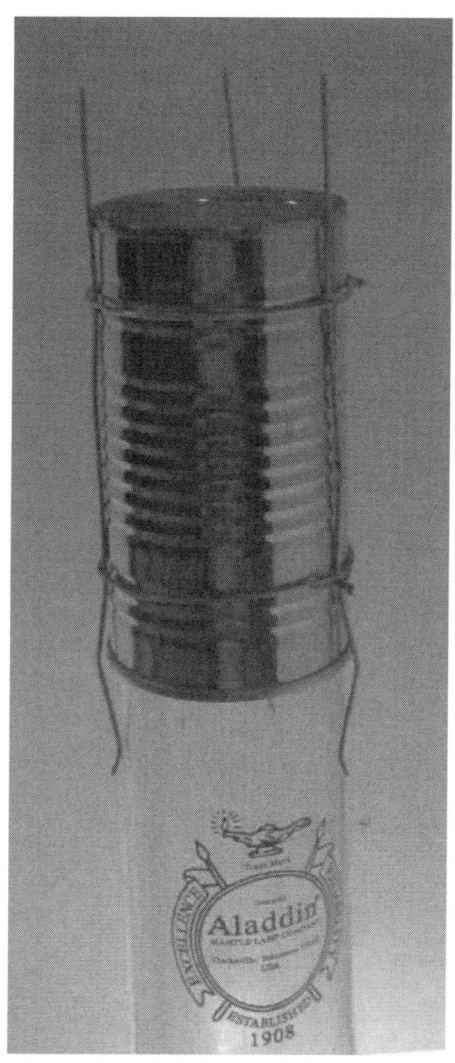

■ **ABOVE:** *Here's the extender mounted on the smaller of the two chimneys. The flange I left in the can lid rests on the glass. Again, the fire-polished bump on the glass guarantees the match-up is far from air tight.* ■

■ **ABOVE:** *The extender in use. Did it work? Yes. I used a Malta-made yttrium mantle. Without the extender it gave 40 watts-worth of light. With the extender it gave 50 watts. Yea team! Note the small, 4" Vise-Grips clamped on the wick wheel. Not only do they provide leverage (i.e. better control), they look pretty dang slick. My wife likes 'em, too. Hands on hips, she said, "Oh, that looks wonderful."* ■

Aladdin Mantles

Page 1, *Aladdin, The Magic Name in Lamps*:

> "In 1905 Johnson first saw the superior light produced by a German kerosene mantle burner, the 'Practicus' . . .

> "Two years later, Victor Johnson gave up his steady job to form the Western Lighting Company in Kansas City, Missouri. The company imported and sold the Practicus . . .

> "In 1908 he changed the [Western Lighting] name and incorporated the Mantle Lamp Company of America.

On page 85, Couter's book displays a full-page ad for the Western Lighting Company. It pictures the Practicus lamp and claims **100** candlepower.

■ **ABOVE:** *Today, 108 years after the Practicus, Aladdin claims* **40** *candlepower.* ■

Light output really has dropped over the years and one reason is the thorium/yttrium issue discussed at the beginning of this book (in the 'Mantles' section of the INTRODUCTION.) Old-time thorium mantles gave more light but were slightly radioactive. Thorium mantles have been replaced almost totally by yttrium mantles.

Another reason for deteriorating performance has to do with machining tolerances and lack of adherence to spec. In the case of Aladdin, some of that resulted from knowhow being lost when moving production between countries.

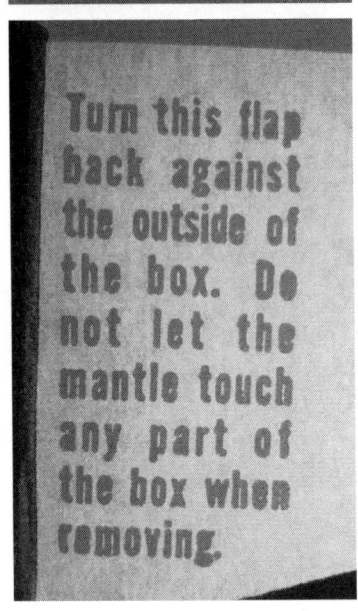

■ **ABOVE:** *In World War II and earlier, Aladdin mantles were made in Chicago. Back then, these mantles were fragile. And, like me, 75 years of aging did not make them stronger. Today, anything you come across from that ancient made-in-USA era is, in simple English, junk. It results from decades of rough handling by people who didn't know what they were doing.* ■

Today, Lehman's cautions its customers (similar to the warning on the old made-in-Chicago box, above), "Don't touch the cloth part before or after you burn off the protective coating." It's good advice. No. *Excellent* advice!

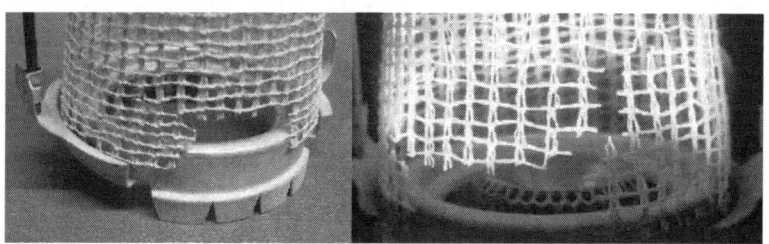

■ **ABOVE:** *A Chicago-made mantle as received from an eBay seller. Damage to a mantle's bottom edge is typical for old US-made and British-made stock. Admittedly, most are better than this (though not by much). The right-hand image shows the same mantle breaking apart ten minutes into its first burn.* ■

■ **ABOVE:** *From 1946-75, mantles were made in the U.K. Shown here is a British-made mantle (a good one) immediately after firing. Note the regularity of the weave. These mantles were thorium and produced 60 watts-worth of light on my Model 23 lamp. This is the kind of product upon which Aladdin built its reputation. Made-in-England mantles have disappeared in the U.S. They're on www.ebay.co.uk/ but they are either rubbish at one end of the spectrum or very expensive at the other.* ■

■ **ABOVE:** *For decades, to avoid government regulations and environmentalist grievances, companies moved non-user-friendly operations to third-world countries. About 1975, Aladdin moved thorium mantle production (radioactive) from the U.K. to Agostini & Co. in Brazil. In this context, camisa means mantle.* ■

Given a regular 12$\frac{1}{2}$" high chimney, my Model 23 lamp produces 40 watts-worth of light with these Brazilian-made thorium mantles.

My Model B produces 50 watts with the same mantle.

My Model 23 produces 60 watts with a Philippine-made yttrium mantle.

I won't attempt to explain WHY the variance exists because I don't fully understand why. I'm simply reporting my own first-hand observations.

■ **ABOVE:** *In 2004, Aladdin again moved mantle production, this time to the 'European Economic Community' (Falks Veritas Ltd, Malta) and switched to non-radioactive yttrium. In theory, the (thorium) Brazilian mantles should produce more light but, in practice, both European and Brazilian mantles produce the same 40 watts on my Model 23 lamp.* ■

Both the Brazilian mantles and the Malta-made mantles are available today on eBay. And they both produce a reliable 40 watts-worth of light.

In 2007, I bought Aladdin mantles for $7.50 each on eBay. At some point after that, production ceased – simply stopped altogether – and mantles grew scarce. In October 2010, I saw one Aladdin mantle sell for $27.96 on eBay. Mantle production resumed in late 2010, this time at Peerless in the Philippines.

We'll discuss the merits of Philippine-made mantles in a moment but, first, think on this. A mere six or seven years ago, production of Aladdin mantles stopped. World-wide. No retailer had them. "Out of stock" was the universal phrase. They vanished from eBay. Could it happen again? Of course. Why not?

Today, Aladdin mantles are made in only one place, the Philippines. There is no alternate source. This is not a situation where The Donald can jump in and yell, "YOU'RE FIRED! I'm moving production to Nigeria. Or Antarctica. Or back to Chicago." *Hey Donald! You do understand the pipeline will be empty for three years, yes?*

Think about government regulations. *Philippine* government regulations. And labor unrest. And floods. And typhoons. Volcanos. *This is the Pacific rim we're talking about.* Earthquakes-Я-Us. My wife is from the Philippines; I know the drill. Seems to me that some judicious hoarding is called for. That plus knowing how to improvise. *Knowledge* is often more valuable than a cache of rusty musty *stuff.*

Improvised Mantles

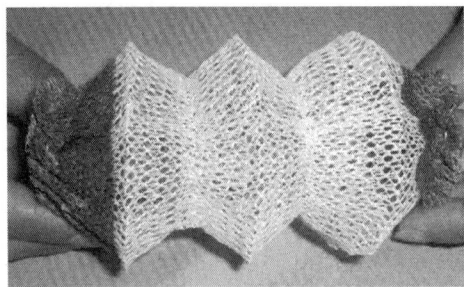

■ **ABOVE:** *A Coleman #95 mantle, designed for the Coleman NorthStar Dual Fuel lantern. It has a hole in each end allowing it to be modified and used on an Aladdin lamp. I've done it. It works. And it throws off 40+ watts-worth of light. As an added bonus, if you begin this project not knowing how to curse, you'll be an expert at the end.* ■

I came across this on www.backwoodshome.com/forum/vb/archive/index.php/t-2516.html:

". . . how to jury-rig a Coleman type 95 mantle. Snip and bend the retaining wire in the #95 mantle to duplicate the [top] opening of an Alladin, then shorten the overall length of the whole mantle by about 1/3. Stretch it out over the round bottum opening, and secure it at the bottom with a length of stiff wire. Hook the retaining wire at the top with those two little hooks that support the top of the mantle. Leave a bit of slack in the mantle because it will contract [shrink] after burning. You'll know there's not enough slack if the mantle tears upon burning." [sic] – Michael

One sentence in those directions sounds easy-breezy but turns out to be extremely challenging: "Stretch it out over the round bottom opening, and secure it at the bottom with a length of stiff wire."

Well hardy, har, har.

Here's my method.

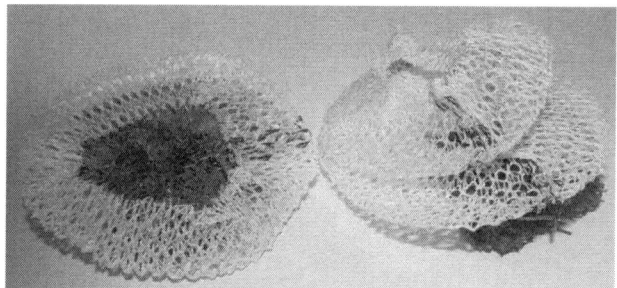

■ **ABOVE:** *First, with scissors, cut off a third of the #95 length. The long section is what we use. The wire loop will form the top; the cut end, the bottom.* ■

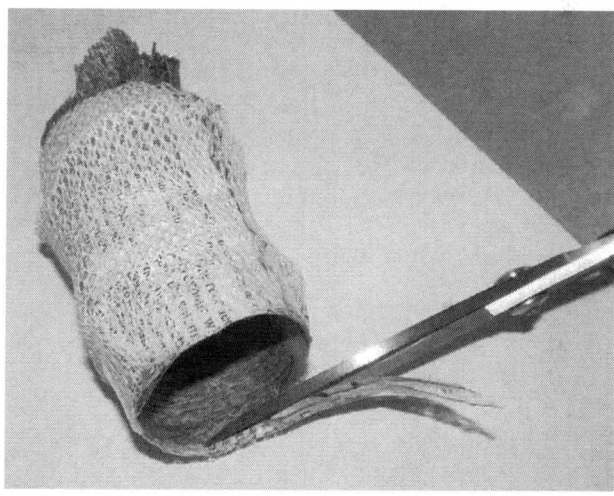

■ **ABOVE:** *Next, tape the cut end of the mantle to a rolled up section of newspaper. First time around, I tried a toilet-paper tube but it was too small in diameter. Match up the cut end of the mantle with the end of the paper tube and then, using short lengths of cellophane tape, wrap the tape from the fabric around to the paper. Finally, trim a smidge off the end (as shown here) and removed the paper. You've tamed the raw, springy edge. We won't use any wire and we won't remove the tape. It will burn off in use.* ■

■ **ABOVE:** *Here's the cloth mantle mounted on the wire frame (and the frame mounted on the gallery and the gallery mounted on the lamp). The bottom of the mantle is stuck to the frame with additional bits of tape. Before mounting it on the gallery, turn the mantle upside down and remove (with cuticle scissors and tweezers) any pieces of tape that block the mantle-frame tabs or spurs. The mantle shown here has been fired. The brownish ring at the bottom is the scorched tape line.* ■

Be gentle! You don't want holes in your finished masterpiece. And the holes won't appear until you fire it.

It does work, but you're gonna ruin a few mantles and spend a few bucks learning how. So do it now while you have the time. Do it now while you have the money. Don't wait until there's a blackout and your wife's water breaks and your firstborn is on its way. Speaking as a man who delivered two babies at home, that's not the best time to begin.

No Mantle at All

You can run an Aladdin without any mantle at all if desired.

The Aladdin has a tubular wick, similar to Rayo or Kosmos or Matador lamps. Raising your Aladdin's flame spreader may improve results (it's something you have to experiment with) but for sure you can get 30 watts-worth of light with no mantle at all.

There's an eight-minute YouTube video (https://www.youtube.com/watch?v=AVBCWe0t5Jg) in which running an Aladdin with no mantle is demonstrated. Note the lamp being demo'd is a Model 12 (1928-1935). The Model 12 was the last center-draft lamp that Aladdin produced. When the Model 12 wick is raised (sans mantle) the video shows a smooth cylinder of flame.

■ **ABOVE:** *All Aladdins after Model 12 are side-draft rather than center-draft. In stark contrast to the video, when I crank up the flame on my Model 23 (sans mantle), four huge spikes of flame appear (located north, south, east, and west), not a smooth cylinder.* ■

In ordinary use (with a mantle), my Model B produces a more uniform circle of flame than does the Model 23. But, after preheating, as you turn up the Model B and peer into its flame, four tiny but distinct spikes appear: north, south, east, west (that is, 90° apart).

Is this phenomenon inherent in the side-burner design? I suspect it is. If you remove the flame spreader and peek down inside the burner, you'll see four baffles. Each model has its own arrangement. I think the intent is to spread the flame uniformly around the circular wick. I suspect it's the baffles that create the flame spikes. The spikes grow as you raise the wick. They ultimately touch the mantle and produce black spots. That's the point at which the lamp tops out. (All of which is pure conjecture on my part.)

The spiking characteristic may concern lamp designers but, to you and me, struggling through a blackout, the real point I'm trying to make is that we can generate 30 watts-worth of light with no mantle at all.

And it's a benchmark of sorts. If your lamp WITH a mantle produces less than 30 watts (36 candlepower), then your mantle is blocking light output, detracting from it, not contributing.

Philippine Mantles

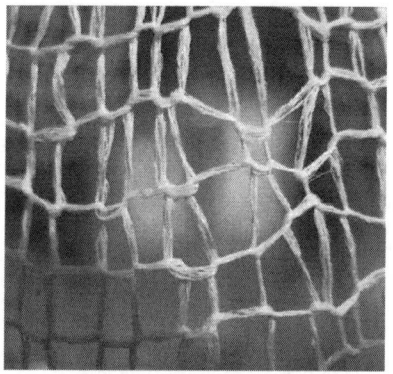

■ **ABOVE:** *This was my **second** Philippine mantle circa 2011. To tell the truth, I was surprised when this yttrium mantle (looking a bit ragged and irregular), produced 40 watts-worth of light on my Model 23 lamp. But that was the upper limit before carbon spots developed.* ■

■ **ABOVE:** *Back in the days of thorium mantles Aladdin lamps wore a tag like this.* ■

■ **ABOVE:** *Today (as printed on the red Philippine mantle box), Aladdin has changed its rating system from watts to candlepower.* ■

Philippine mantles claim 40 *candlepower* on the box which equates to 33.5 *watts*. Gee, we can get 30 watts without a mantle. Yes, there's higher fuel usage and yes, there's more kerosene smell, but, if 40 *candlepower* is truly all we can get, then we're uncomfortably close to the point where we'd be just as well off with no mantle at all.

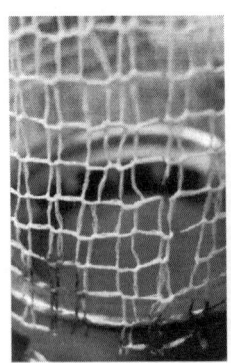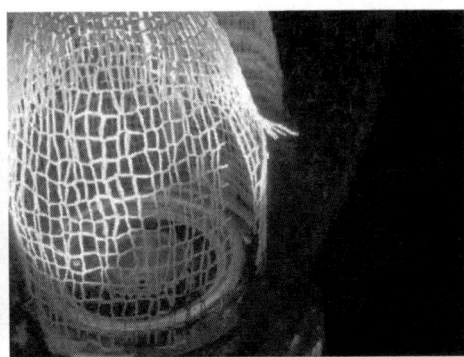

■ **ABOVE:** *Earlier I pictured my **second** Philippine mantle. But here's my **first** (again, it dates from the 2010-2011 era). Straight out of the box there were breaks in the weave. In use, such mantles self-destruct.* ■

But how are Philippine mantles today? Ah! The $64 dollar question.

In 2015 Galen Lehman wrote me, "Aladdin Industries did not save complete documentation on how to make mantles. As production was moved from country to country, critical pieces of information were lost. Sam [i.e. Sam Blank, owner of Gasman Mantle Mfg. Corp. in the Philippines who currently makes Aladdin mantles] is the hero here. Since he started without adequate information . . . The current mantles do have consistent shape, knitting, coating and light output."

As it turns out, by my testing, it's the boxes that need to be updated; the mantles inside the boxes are outstanding. Philippine mantles made in 2014 produced 60 watts-worth of light on my Model 23 burner. Not too shabby.

But although today's mantles pass muster (that is, the mantles *produced* today), the cynic in me believes that mantles produced yesterday (old stuff) is still lurking in sellers' inventories. And how do you, the customer, specify '*send me only new production*' on your order blank?

So I performed a little test, ordering a couple of Aladdin mantles from a trusted seller, a man from whom I've several times purchased lantern parts in the past. He's an active dealer and I expected him to have a respectable inventory turnover rate.

Unfortunately, my fears were confirmed. The Philippine mantles I ordered (and received) in August 2015 had breaks in the fabric right out of the box. The breaks could not be seen before firing due to the blue coating. The mantles were as bad as anything I saw back in 2010-11 and they broke apart in use. Old inventory for sure. And there are no date codes to steer us around old inventory. Bummer.

Ah! Here's some late-breaking news. Good news. (1) The standard red box for Philippine-made mantles, used until now, will indicate mantles made pre-2015. (2) The same box with 'Crownplace Brands' printed on it will indicate 2015 production. (3) Future production runs will have "a lot number and/or year of manufacture on them." Wow! Pinch me. *Somebody is listening!*

Mantle Recommendations

1. Don't buy any made-in-Chicago Aladdin mantles. They are ancient. They are fragile. They are certain to be damaged. Damaged mantles self-destruct when you put fire to them.

2. Made-in-England mantles are similar. Most look seriously old with rusty harps. They'll never survive an ocean voyage or airport baggage handlers. Made-in-England mantles of a higher caste are sometimes available and will produce 60 watts-worth of light but are pricey.

For example, today's U.S. 'Buy-it-now' price (www.ebay.com) is $13.25 with shipping included for one Philippine-made yttrium mantle.

Today's U.K. 'Buy-it-now' price (www.ebay.co.uk) is $29.22 (U.S. dollars) with shipping included for one British-made thorium mantle. These mantles are no longer made; have not been made for 40 years; will never be made again. They are a consumable item. Tomorrow's price will be higher.

3. Brazilian-made and Malta-made mantles are both, by my reckoning, 40-watt mantles. Both can be found on eBay and both are consistent performers. The 'Malta-made' box is marked "Made in the European Community."

4. Today's Philippine-made mantles are 60-watt mantles. I recommend you buy them *only* direct from Lehman's (https://www.lehmans.com/). Lehman's is a major player; its inventory turnover is high; that means you'll get mantles that were recently produced. (In the interest of full disclosure, please know I have zero financial interest in Lehman's.)

In every case, no matter what Aladdin mantle you buy or where it's from, open every box and check every mantle individually. I have received shattered mantles in perfect boxes from trusted sellers. On eBay, buy only from sellers with a 100% satisfaction rating from their customers.

Galen Lehman advises, "Lehman's (and most reliable retailers) will replace mantles that arrive to customers broken." And that's great. Except what I have done is to buy a dozen mantles in one shot, receive them neatly packed in a carton, check one and, finding that one to be okay, set the entire box on a shelf. Ten years later (after I've long since forgotten who the vendor was) I discover that some of the mantles in that carton are not so good. So, again, check them individually when first received.

Your mantle choices are USA, England, Brazil, Malta, and Philippines. A reasonable expectation with Brazilian-made and Malta-made mantles is 40 watts-worth of light. With NEW Philippine production, you can expect 60 watts. That's equivalent to the performance standard of yesteryear; doubly impressive because today's mantles are yttrium, not thorium.

Mantle Storage

If you must for some reason violate recommendation #4, above, and buy Philippine-made mantles outside Lehman's, then I suggest you buy only one and try it out before investing in a dozen that may or may not be any good.

Problem is, if you already have a good mantle mounted on your Aladdin, fired and operational, how do you store that one while testing a second one? Aladdin mantles are a bit expensive to toss in the trash (!) yet extremely delicate to store if they've already been fired.

Here's what I do. A wide-mouth pint canning jar from m'lady's pantry works well. Just add a stick-on mailing label to describe what it's all about. (Because you won't remember. Trust me.) And put it high on a shelf where it won't get bumped or jostled. Somewhere you won't forget.

In my case, that last bit guarantees I'll never see it again.

Safety

We haven't yet discussed safety. Aladdins are rather fickle creatures with a reputation for 'running high' (i.e. the flame gradually creeps up, higher and higher, until it gives trouble).

If you research Aladdin lamps on lamper forums and camper forums, you'll see one piece of advice repeated again and again and again. *Never leave your Aladdin unattended.* Your *burning* Aladdin, of course.

Couldn't have said it better myself.

Never leave your Aladdin unattended.

If an Aladdin goes runaway, "turn it down and place a plate [or saucer] on top the chimney, it will go out." http://www.backwoodshome.com/forum/vb/showthread.php?t=924

Great! But how do you "turn it down" when the wick wheel burns your fingers? I mean **BURNS** your fingers. Answer. Keep some pliers handy. In addition, I personally keep some supple leather gardening gloves right beside the pliers and the Pyrex saucer. The gloves will serve as potholders if need be.

Nor will it hurt to show a second person in the house how to handle the situation.

Aladdin lamps can be fickle critters. Repeat after me: *Never leave your Aladdin unattended.*

Test Results Recap

■ **ABOVE:** *This is my Model 23 'star' lamp (touted by J.W. Courter). By my testing (with a regular 12¹/₂" tall chimney) it produces **40** watts-worth of light with a Brazilian mantle; **40** watts with a Malta-made mantle; and **60** watts with a 2014 Philippine mantle. Your mileage may vary. The Model 23 burner, star or not, is legendary for inconsistent performance, lamp-to-lamp.* ■

■ **ABOVE:** *This is my Model B burner ("held out as 'the best' by many collectors" per Galen Lehman). By my testing (with a regular 12½" tall chimney) it produces **40** watts-worth of light with a Brazilian mantle; **50** watts with a Malta-made mantle; and **60** watts with a 2014 Philippine mantle.* ■

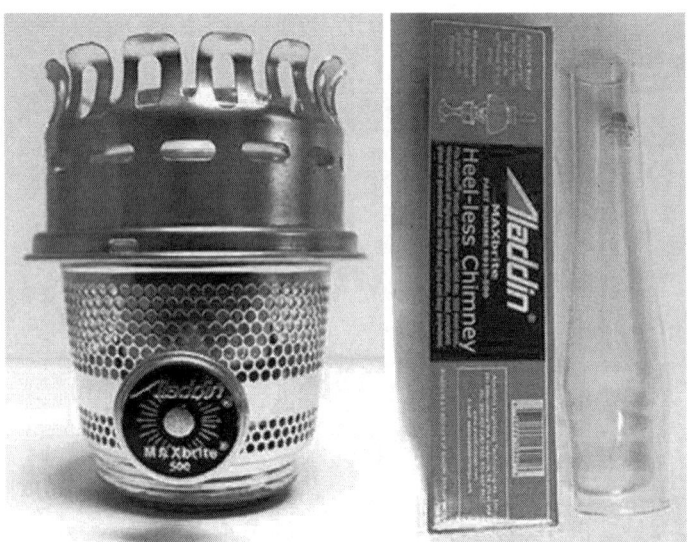

■ **ABOVE:** *And [drumroll please] here's the MAXbrite 500 burner, the first new Aladdin model in 46 years, coming soon to a Lehman's catalog near you. (Note that it takes a heel-less chimney, not a Lox-On.)* ■

"Yea team! *One thousand candlepower!*"

"A *thousand?* No. Is that really what he said?"

"Yeah. I think so. At least that's what *I* heard. And not only that. I heard the new ones come with a genie and three wishes. Can you believe it?"

Printed in Great Britain
by Amazon

16806414R00097